BLASKET MEMORIES

THE LIFE OF AN IRISH ISLAND COMMUNITY

Edited by
PÁDRAIG TYERS

MERCIER PRESS

IRISH AMERICAN BOOK COMPANY (IABC)
Boulder, Colorado

MERCIER PRESS
PO Box 5, 5 French Church Street, Cork
16 Hume Street, Dublin 2

Trade enquiries to CMD DISTRIBUTION,
55a Spruce Avenue, Stillorgan Industrial Park, Blackrock, Dublin

Published in the US and Canada by the
IRISH AMERICAN BOOK COMPANY
6309 Monarch Park Place, Niwot, Colorado, 80503
Tel: (303) 652 2710, (800) 452-7115
Fax: (303) 652 2689, (800) 401-9705

First published in Irish, *Leoithne Aniar,* in 1982.

© Pádraig Tyers, 1998

ISBN 1 85635 230 7

10 9 8 7 6 5 4 3 2 1

Printed in Ireland by Colour Books Ltd.

BLASKET MEMORIES

FOREWORD

I first set foot on the Great Blasket Island in July 1948, exactly fifty years ago and five years before it was finally evacuated. At that time the island community amounted to about twenty-eight people, many of them in the twilight of their lives. Through subsequent years I struck up with them a firm friendship which I cherish.

Though many books had been written about the Blasket and its people it was clear that a great fund of knowledge and lore still remained to be collected and preserved and without undue delay too as one by one the islanders were going to their eternal reward. Consequently in the late 1960s and early 1970s I set about recording on tape the memories of both the surviving islanders and others who were not natives of the Blasket but were closely connected with it in one way or another.

Then in the mid-1970s I learned of the existence of a manuscript written by Seán Ó Criomhthain whose father Tomás was author of the internationally acclaimed *An tOileánach*. Tragically Seán had died a few years earlier but his daughter Niamh Bean Uí Laoithe very kindly made the manuscript available to me, and for that I am indebted to her.

This book therefore consists of Seán Ó Criomhthain's manuscript (pp. 7–88) and the transcript of a number of interviews recorded on tape by me. Of the four people whom I interviewed three have passed away, a bed in heaven to them. Thankfully Seán Ó Guithín is still hale and hearty and resides in Dunquin. I hope that this book will help to perpetuate their memories.

I am grateful to Radio Telefís Éireann and to University College Cork for permission to publish material included here. Finally I owe a particular debt of gratitude to Cló Dhuibhne (Baile an Fheirtéaraigh) who in 1982 published *Leoithne Aniar* and graciously allowed me to translate it into English under the title of *Blasket Memories*.

PÁDRAIG TYERS

1

These islands were named after the Ferriters up to seven hundred years ago. The proof of this is that there's a promontory near the pier which is called Castle Point. Piaras Feirtéar had a castle there. His hideout known as Piaras' Cave is in the middle of the Great Island on the north-western side and one would need to know every inch of the island well to find it. You would also need a good head on you to get down to it. That's where Piaras used to hide when being hunted, as indeed he often was. Even so he didn't end his days on the Western Island. That's another story altogether.

The Ferriter clan was on the Island before ever Piaras arrived. He is praised and criticised for his deeds both good and bad. There's a rock on the northern side of Inishtooskert called the Sailors' Rock and any time a ship passed by which Piaras suspected of having valuables on board he would attack it and carry off the whole cargo. He landed the sailors from one of these boats on the rock which has ever since been known as the Sailors' Rock.

Life on the Western Island was always hard, miserable and very poor before Piaras' time and ever since, and I promise you that nobody in this world realises that except those who were compelled by need to go to live there. There's a lot to be told about them.

There are old habitations on those islands but there's no account, either written or oral, as to the identity or place of origin of the people who left their traces after them. Some people say that the Norsemen were the ones responsible for the distinct mark which is to be seen on the Great Island today. They accomplished great work there and if you ever happen to set foot on the Blasket you will see the signs of their labours. Long ago if the children were out late at night and met some old man he would tell them to go home fast, that the Norsemen were coming eastwards from Goods Strand. The children would then run home hotfoot.

This last line of people to live on the Island went there not more than two hundred years ago, if it is even that much. They went there from the parish of Ventry, from Dunquin and from the parish of Ballyferriter, not because of high spirits nor on holidays. It was the very opposite. Want, hunger and poverty caused them to go there. The Kearneys and the O'Sullivans came there from Raheens in the parish of Ventry, the O'Sheas and the O'Dunleaveys from the same parish also, the O'Connors and the O'Crohans from the parish of Dunquin and the Keanes from the parish of Ballyferriter. I'm not certain as to where the O'Guiheens came from but they are said to be the first group that went there. Those are the families who lived on the Island until it was abandoned.

The Earl of Cork was at that time the landlord of the Island and there was a nice old Irish saying that had to do with that same earl. 'Food for your child,' as an old man said, 'and rent for the landlord,' and if anyone had that to say it was the islanders. The only thing in their favour was that the landing-place there was better than any on the other islands. They brought livestock in with them, cows, donkeys, horses, sheep, goats, dogs, cats and any other animals which they required. They had large boats, each with a crew of eight, and without those eight men it was impossible to knock a stir out of the boat. There was no proper landing-place in Dunquin itself, only what was called a rocky foreshore, in Bealaha and Fileclea. By all accounts there was a lot of boats in Fileclea itself and it was difficult to land there depending on the weather. It is said that every man who went to live on the Island then was over six feet tall and broad and strong accordingly. They needed to be, otherwise they would never have survived there.

The people who went to live on the Island and their mainland relatives worked hand in hand. Those on the Island would send out word whenever they needed anything and a horse and cart would be waiting outside to bring them wherever they wished to go.

There are three other islands quite close to the Great Island, Beginish, Inishtooskert and the biggest one of them Inishvickillane. It is said that there's no account whatsoever as to when the house on Beginish was built, nor can any inhabitant of the Great Island remember it. Traces of that house are clearly visible today but it wasn't at all like those on the Great Island. To judge by the ruins still there it was a fine spacious house, and was said to be roofed with slate.

Beginish is a low-lying level island with no shelter or protection from the weather. Consequently no signs of tillage remain. It contains turf which however is not suitable as fuel because the salt-water flows in over this little island every winter and remains in the turf. There's no fresh water in any part of it but as it is only a quarter of a mile from the Great Island the people living there used to come over to where there was a fine fresh water well. They brought the fresh water back with them in small barrels. That well has ever since been known as the Well at Keereelach's Point, because tradition tells us that Keereelach was the name of the man living in the house on Beginish, having been sent there as a cattle herd by some fellow from England. It is said that it had the grass of forty cows, and a boat used to serve Keereelach bringing provisions to him and taking cattle away according as they were ready.

There is another island called Inishtooskert, quite a large one that had plenty of grazing for cattle. There was a big population on the Great Island when people went to live on Inishtooskert. Those people from the Great Island rented Inishtooskert and sent one of their own men and his wife to live there. It has no suitable landing place for boats, but because it is sheltered it is easy to land there unless of course the sea is swollen.

The people on the Great Island had to look after the herdsman and provide him with everything he required. There was an underground cabin on Inishtookert. It is still there, a sort of sheep-hut roofed with stone. It is quite large, round-shaped and roughly twenty feet across. There are stone steps, or a stairs as you might say, going down into it, and that stairs is about eight feet wide. When the man on this rock urgently needed anything the agreed signal between him and those on the Great Island was to light a bundle of hay outside the door of the hut. They were always on the lookout for that signal. Things were going very well and whatever they did or did not do the thought of the land-steward or of paying the rent never entered their heads.

One day Clara Hussey and the bailiffs came but the herdsman had spotted the bailiffs' boat leaving the Narrow Water Harbour. He lit his bundle of hay, and assistance from the

Western Island reached him before the bailiffs who weren't allowed even to land. The battle fought on Inishtooskert that day put an end forever to bailiffs, and it also put an end to the man acting as a herdsman there.

There is another large rock directly west of the Great Island. It is known as the Tearaght. No grass grows there, only a kind of weeds and patches of cliff-grass and thrift here and there. Goats, however, were plentiful on the Great Island and as soon as the young goats were a couple of months old the islanders brought them west there so as to have them fit to kill as one year-olds. There wasn't a rock above sea-level that the islanders didn't have a goat or a sheep on it. When the time came to bring goats back from the Tearaght the islanders went to fetch them. They were really delighted at the thought of having a good barrelful of salted goat-meat for the year. However things don't always turn out as expected, and so it was with the islanders. Eight men were landed on the rock and two others stayed on board to mind the boat. If they were to keep chasing the goats to this very day their task would have been in vain. Those young goats had become wild, and were seven times wilder if a person approached them. The men failed completely to catch even one of them, and there was never since such a day of cursing and swearing, each man cursing the other.

'They returned home,' said the old woman, 'without as much as a goat's whisker.'

Soon the rock was teeming with goats and there was nobody to interfere with them. But goats too don't always have things their own way. The lighthouse men then came to build the lighthouse, some forty of them, with all sorts of equipment. Whenever they needed a goat they had a gun handy with which to shoot and kill it. Before the light on the Tearaght was lit there wasn't a goat to be seen there. They had all been killed and eaten.

There is another island to the south of the Great Blasket which is called Inishvickillane and consists of up to two hundred acres. Nobody knows its history except for the folklore connected with it. There were two dwellings there – one of them is still to the good – and there was a herdsman in each of them, one man on duty by night and the other by day. The remains of a church known as the Little Old Chapel survive and what is still to be seen of it shows excellent workmanship.

People inhabited Inishvickillane before the Great Famine but the story goes that it was unoccupied for some time afterwards. The Earl of Cork had a steward on it who used to bring the cattle there and also hired the two herdsmen. He supplied all their needs because he arranged for a boat from the Great Island belonging to relatives of theirs to serve them. The herdsmen had their wives and families with them and also a small boat to bring them in and out wherever they wished to go. The people on the Great Island envied them greatly because they didn't have to buy anything and had nine pounds a year from the steward to put in their pockets. They were free to sow and reap as much as they wished, and had two milk-cows and as many sheep and cattle as they desired. They grew a lot of oats as well as potatoes and onions and many other vegetables too. On the other hand they had to be out at all times of the night guarding them because the rabbits used to do great damage to the crops, but they didn't mind. They had the help and were eager to work.

This island was for many years under the control of the steward. It produced top quality stock, big heavy cattle and fine fat sheep. Whenever a herdsman gave up the job or became too old the steward would send a relative of his as a replacement. The island is said to have been much frequented by the good people, or fairies as they are known, but whatever fairies or pookas were being seen there the herdsman was obliged to be out until daybreak. That was their responsibility and they had to fulfil it.

There is a tune or air still to be heard quite often around here. It is called the 'Fairy Tune'. It had never before been heard anywhere until it was heard in Inishvickillane by one of the herdsmen as he tended the cattle one night. There are no words to go with the air.

There is also a song called 'My Katty and I will go Strolling'. If the folklore connected with it is true a herdsman in Inishvickillane was married to a slipshod woman who was no great beauty whereas he himself was very good-looking indeed. Another herdsman on the island at that same time had the finest-looking woman in Ireland but he himself was no oil-painting. It

11

is said that the good-looking man and the beautiful woman were often in conversation together and his wife became suspicious that he was lying with her too often. Such things do happen and happened in this instance. One fine sunny morning as the beautiful woman's husband was looking out to sea what should he notice only a woman on the crest of the wave singing the song 'My Katty and I will go Strolling'. He returned home and told his wife about it. She went to the other house, and if she did the shipshod woman was nowhere to be seen. They launched their little boat and went out to the spot on the sea where the woman had been but there was neither trace nor tidings of her.

There was a lot of talk about this woman's disappearance as there is about everything that goes wrong. She had no family and it is said that she and her husband were very upset because of not having an heir to replace them on the island and that consequently they would be obliged to leave when they got old.

When the tragedy occurred a bundle of hay was lit. That was the signal in time of emergency. The burning hay was seen from the Great Island and it wasn't long before the service-boat was launched and went west. When it reached Inishvickillane the crew found the husband of the missing woman very upset. They were informed of what had happened and were told that she had been floating on the water just as if she was sitting by the fireside singing that song. Two of the men from the boat stayed three weeks on the island to see if there was any chance of the body being found. The service-boat called to the island twice a week during those three weeks but the tide around Inishvickillane is very strong, and if the corpse surfaced the tide would carry it away unless of course it surfaced during daylight. It has never since been found. The event led to much talk and everyone had his own version.

Some time after the three weeks had elapsed the man in question left the island and there has been no account ever since as to where he went. The steward of Inishvickillane heard about the matter and about the carry-on of the drowned woman's husband and after thinking it over he decided never again to send a second married couple to Inish. One herdsman had to fulfil all the duties from that on but he got double pay.

Everything turns out well in due course and grace comes

with patience. No matter how long the scab is on a wound it disappears with the passage of time. That is exactly how it was on Inishvickillane. Soon the memory of the tragedy was no more and people forgot that such an event had ever occurred. The herdsman continued on minding and tending the stock. The steward in charge of Inish used to bring a trawler from Dingle about the beginning of November and take off all the fattened animals. He often had to make two journeys to remove all the fattened stock before the coming of winter. That was the situation for many years. When the family left Inish the herdsman also had to leave with them and come to the Great Blasket to live out the rest of his days there. The steward appointed his nearest relative to replace him and that man was glad to leave the Great Island as it was easier for him to make a living on Inish because he had his food for nothing from the steward.

That situation prevailed from generation to generation, as the man said. One particular herdsman had with him his wife, his family of five and two lads from the Great Island whom he had brought with him for help and company. They still had the small boat and this herdsman used to go to Dingle in it all on his own. The story goes that he went to Dingle one day and from the time he left Inish until he reached the mouth of Dingle Harbour he saw a road running beside the boat all the way. Nobody paid any attention to his story. In fact they only made fun of him, but it seems he wasn't given to lying. Indeed it was always said that he never uttered a word of a lie. The matter rested so for a time but he always continued to talk about the road.

There was always a man on the hill of the Great Island herding cattle and hunting rabbits. Quite early one morning he went to a spot where he had a view of Inish and noticed a fire and smoke. The fire was the recognised distress signal. He rushed home at once and announced that he had seen the distress signal on Inish. The rescue boat was got ready and it set out west with all possible speed.

The herdsman's wife was waiting for them as they reached the landing-place and the news she had for them was anything but good. Her husband and the two lads whom he had brought with him to Inish a few weeks previously were missing without trace. She told them that when she had last seen them they were pollack-fishing around the Warrior Rock, a submerged reef. Then the hullabaloo commenced. There was nothing they could do but bring his wife and five children back from Inish to her parents' home where they would be amongst relatives. The three bodies were never recovered. She then told everyone how her husband had often spoken of the road which a few years previously he had seen beside him as he was on his way east from Inish to the mouth of Dingle Harbour, and that he always maintained that it was the road that would lead himself to heaven.

Apparitions do occur and foretell certain future events. The dead cannot sustain the living, and so the steward came and gave the job as herdsman to the dead man's sister who was married to a man from the Island. He also gave her the responsibility of caring for the family who had been left fatherless. The widow and her family lived on the Great Island from that time onwards.

2

The Earl of Cork was landlord of the Western Island but people suffered not so much at his hands as at the hands of his stewards.

There was a bitch of a steward, as the islanders used to say, to the north of them and another bitch to the south. Bess Rice was the one to the south where she had the parish of Ventry rented out, while Clara Hussey was to the north and had the parish of Ballyferriter rented out. Clara was so hard on the islanders that they were obliged to join together to fight her.

If an islander was unable to pay the rent on time she would send in the bailiffs. They would remove everything they could lay hands on, and perhaps there might be nothing there belonging to the man who hadn't paid the rent. She also had a scout on the Island and his duty was to bring her a weekly report detailing the number of rabbits and sea-birds and puffins they had killed that week. A dozen rabbit-skins would fetch a good price in Dingle in those days and it was those skins that paid the rent for them.

The scout approached the islanders on one occasion and informed them that they would no longer be permitted to kill as many rabbits as they wished but rather so many dozen according to the size of each one's holding. On hearing this the islanders were extremely angry. Their blood began to boil and they became enraged. From then on there was dissension between themselves and the steward. It is also said that the scout himself didn't escape, that he was thrown overboard when being ferried out to Dunquin with a batch of reports for the steward.

However every tide no matter how high has to recede. The islanders carried on as best they could. They had to put up with landlords and stewards, rent, bailiffs, killing and exhaustion, but they never gave up the battle and continued on. The steward had failed to collect as much as a halfpenny of rent, but whatever complaints he made to the landlord didn't the landlord attack them with vigour and force! They approached the Island in a gunboat firing shots from their guns into the air.

The islanders moved neither hand nor foot. The bailiffs in the gunboat attempted to load the sheep and other animals into their boat but alas and alack! They didn't have the know-how with the result that they had to give up the battle of their own accord. Not even bullets could force wild sheep down into a place where they weren't used to going. The bailiffs were so frustrated that they fired at the sheep and killed a few, but when their leader saw the shots being fired he called a halt. He was left with no option but to order his men to take away the islanders' boats, both big and small, which were on the pier. In doing so they met with no resistance because the poor islanders were in dread of the guns. Were it not for that I assure you that there would have been rivers of red blood on the island landing-place that day. The gunboat towed the boats away, but where they brought them I cannot say.

The leader and the bailiffs who had accompanied him presumed that they had left the islanders without a single boat, and that consequently they would have to pay the rent whether they liked it or not. They were mistaken, however, because there were two other landing-places on the Island, the Boat Cove and Goods Strand, in each of which the islanders kept one of their large boats. When the gunboat dropped its anchor those two boats were out of sight because they were on the northern side. Word spread that the landlords and the stewards had left the islanders without boats and the people on the mainland were absolutely furious. They set out on foot from door to door to collect some money and the neighbours generously contributed according to their means. It wasn't long until two other large boats were sent to the islanders to replace those lost.

Some of the islanders longed for peace and wished to pay the rent but they were afraid of the others who held that the rent was too high and shouldn't be paid since there was neither a road nor a path to the Island except the blue sea. Nobody broke ranks until they were granted a reduction in the rent, so that, as the man said, two rabbits would pay the rent for him today. However before they succeeded in doing so they had survived many attacks and had spilt red blood. There were brave men on the Island at that time but they couldn't compare with the women who wouldn't take long to collect a heap of stones as ammunition.

The bailiffs were all the time keeping an eye on the islanders and if they happened to come upon one of them on the pier at Dunquin they would take everything he possessed off him. They were empowered by the law to do so but any day the bailiffs arrived at the pier the islanders would get wind of the word from someone in Dunquin warning them not to come out for any goods until the bailiffs had left the scene.

It frequently occurred that the islanders went out for provisions and were on the pier before the bailiff arrived. If he arrived while they were still there they couldn't bring anything home with them because as soon as he saw what they were carrying it was just a case of 'Leave that there or pay your rates!' But that rarely occurred because the people of Dunquin would bring all their goods down to the pier to them and the bailiff was powerless to touch those people as he had no warrant against them. The islanders would hop into the nayvogue on the water because a bailiff cannot interfere with anything afloat. Then the Dunquin people would load all the goods into the nayvogue without an islander as much as laying a hand on anything. One of the Dunquin men would then say to the crew: 'Bring this into poor Pad and that into old Máire' and so on. They were too smart for the bailiff and he had to put away his arms and head off home for himself. Bailiffs and the maintenance of arms to keep an eye on poor unfortunate people living on a sea-rock were a costly business.

It must be said that the islanders resisted very bravely the bailiffs and the rent and rate collectors. They stood shoulder to shoulder. The rent collectors gave up after the big bailiff from Ballyferriter was nearly killed as he returned home in his boat. Clara Hussey's men in Ballyferriter stopped collecting of their own accord, and a rate collector came soon afterwards but I imagine that he lost more than he gained from his efforts and he finally threw in the towel.

A man from Dunquin took on the task then but he would have been better off not to have got involved because he got a hammering from relatives of the islanders living in Dunquin. He too had to give up in a hurry and should be very grateful that he wasn't killed one fair-day in Dingle. A second man from Dunquin took his place and went very close to having his house burned down but after he received the warning he made no further move.

From that time onwards rate demands were made by post. That suited the tricksters on the Island fine. The islanders had always held that they shouldn't have been paying rent or rates since no road nor path was being maintained for them, that their only road was one which was watching its chance to drown them even on the finest day that ever came. An islandman said that the greatest hardships are overcome the fastest. They had learned from those who preceded them and even the mouth of the gun held no great terror for them. The Island has been free from rent and rates ever since but I can't say if it will continue to be so. Nobody can foretell what the future holds.

At the beginning of this century the islanders were doing well even though they had little wealth but the Island itself was in a bad shape. There was neither fence nor bush nor any means of identifying anyone's holding other than a stone to mark the bottom and top of each field and the width of a couple of ridges between every two stones. The young lads often came and moved the stones, an action which frequently caused blood-spilling. Some people's houses were in a terrible state and even the finest one on the Island then was no better than a pig-sty.

The parish priest at the time got to work and wrote to John Bull's government and as a result of his requests and demands the government arranged that the Island become the responsibility of the Congested Districts Board. A gentleman came in one day with a tent. He set up the tent and when he was ready for action he asked for some small sticks. After they were provided he got two men and began to mark out the land according to the map which he had. The marks and stones which had been the cause of argument and trouble were removed and the sticks which this fellow had were placed much further apart. Having completed that task he went out to Dingle and ordered wire and large timber stakes. He hired a trawler there and filled it to the top.

All that was needed now was a favourable wind. There were no engines in the Dingle trawlers in those days nor any mention of them. The captain of this large boat was a man named Brosnan, and he and his crew spent many a day and night in Dingle Bay waiting for a favourable wind. The wind wasn't the greatest problem but rather the strong tide in the Blasket Sound and without sufficient wind he would be unable to anchor off the Island's strand. If he could reach the anchorage with his cargo he would be very pleased with himself because he was an easy-going man who accepted life's fortunes. At last he reached the anchorage and the islanders spent two days and two nights unloading the wire and stakes.

Every man capable of doing a day's work was employed within a week and the Board's pay at the time was two shillings a day. The islanders found no fault with that. What alternative had they? The man from the Board built a road down to the Gravel Strand and got all the donkeys on the Island to bring gravel to the cliff-top where it was unloaded. The gravel was brought up in bags and each donkey carried roughly a hundred-weight. When enough gravel had been brought up he stopped. He then began erecting a high fence all around the village so that neither sheep nor any other animal could encroach on the land under tillage. He put a pulley and three rows of wire on top of the fence and also a couple of fine gates.

The work continued on and when the fences were complet-ed he commenced the building of the new houses. Not many of the islanders accepted these houses because if they wished to have one built for them they themselves would have to draw the gravel from the top of the strand to the site. It is said that necessity is the mother of invention, and those whose old hous-es were about to fall down around them went out to the main-land and got donkey-carts from relatives. They brought them in and set about drawing the gravel from the strand.

The work on the Island took a year and eight months. With the coming of summer the fishermen started lobster-fishing and the boss was left with only a handful of old people and young lads who had just left school. He didn't worry as long as he had two or three working for him because he himself was happy as could be there. He was from County Mayo and hadn't a word of Irish in his mouth. There was a middle-aged man on the Island who had a good smattering of English and was able to read and write it, and the boss appointed him as a sort of ganger. Nevertheless the ganger was required to work like everyone else. It was then that another islander remarked: 'His English didn't do him much good. He is stuck in the gutter the same as myself.'

3

The Western Island was for many years full of wild birds until the young people who had grown up learned how to catch them. There were two kinds of hawk, the big one and the medium-sized one. There was the *dónall dubh*, known to some people as the raven, and the eagle which was the largest of all. It is said that when the Ferriters were in possession of the Island long ago they wished the rent to be paid in the form of young hawks.

The hawk was the most hunted of the birds but I can't really say exactly how many chicks each hawk had. There was a man in Dingle who used to buy the hawks both young and old and pay a good price for them. As a man from Dunquin said, an islandman would go to hell for a penny's worth. Hawks' nests were rarely to be found and any nest that was found proved quite difficult to reach. Sometimes it was impossible. There was a hawk's nest on every island and as soon as the young were preparing to leave the nest the islanders pounced on them. Those hawks and the ravens used to play havoc with the other small sea-birds around the Island, and it was on those small birds that the islanders depended for food and for fine warm down to put under them in bed, not to mention the young puffin, the chick which they regularly had on the table as food, either fresh or salted. The raven was a problem in another way too. If when sheep were lambing there was a raven within twenty miles of one of them he would be on the spot before the lamb was half-born, and would carry off every bit of the lamb and the afterbirth.

There is a spot in Inishtooskert called the Standing Stones and there is a channel of water between it and the land. A nayvogue could easily get through that channel. High up above a bridge links the Standing Stones and the Island, and anyone with a good head for heights could get to the top. It is four hundred feet from the water to the top of the rock which stands straight up as erect as the pole on the Tearaght Lighthouse. To look upwards from the water you'd swear that not even a cat could reach the top so frightening does it look. In olden days the eagles used to nest on its highest point and no man born on the

Island ever even considered climbing up there. They felt it was impossible, and then of course there was the fear of the eagle.

There were two men from the northern slope of the Parish O'Moore who from morning to night used to fish for pollack in their nayvogue, bring the fish home, cure it and sell it at the monthly fish market in Dingle. They used to traverse the whole sea in search of those pollack because it is difficult to find them except on certain fishing-banks. Every fine morning they would set out from Brandon Creek in the north and if the pollack weren't biting they would continue on rowing out as far as the Tearaght, not to mention Barralea, and if there were no pollack on that bank their day's work was in vain unless some turned up in the evening. Each man had two fishing-lines which were tied around his thigh, and the fellow manoeuvring the nayvogue would catch a pollack as well as the next. That is how they spent each summer going west to the islands and back again and their knowledge of the area equalled that of the islanders.

Those two men set out from Brandon Creek early one fine morning with their fishing gear and food on board. The end of the summer was approaching by this time with every young bird fully fledged and ready to leave the nest. They were heading steadily west because a boat fishing for pollack doesn't move fast. They got as far as the Raven, a rock which is a short distance out from Sybil Head but if they did no fish was biting. There was nothing to do but head for Barralea because if there were pollack near the surface of the water anywhere they would surely be there. Off they went west and in no time at all the pollack started to bite. They caught twenty within ten minutes but the pollack then lost their appetite because they had been on the surface since dawn.

The day was very calm and the water like glass and they said they would try again at low tide. They went into the Mooring Cove and moored the nayvogue. They took out their bit of food for the day. It was anything but skimpy because they were two powerful men engaged in heavy work and couldn't carry out their difficult task unless their stomachs were full.

There is an old hovel on this island and they were well aware that it contained tins and saucepans and cooking apparatus. They picked out a large-sized pollack sufficient to feed four men and up they went into the hovel where there was no end of dry heather bushes. The two were experts at cooking and they stuffed more food than five men could eat into their stomachs. After that they smoked their fill. Later on when they finished relaxing after the meal one of them remarked to the other that eagle-chicks were fetching a hell of a price if only a fellow could lay hands on one.

They got ready immediately and set out in search of the eagle in Standing Stones. They went off up the hill and then down the cliff bringing with them the required cliff gear which consisted of just a good strong sack and a piece of fairly sound rope. They crossed over the bridge and made to go up to the top which was quite frightening above the sea. I'm afraid the two 'cats' weren't at all daunted by the fearsome cliff. Their greatest fear was that the mother-eagle would arrive before they could complete their task. One of them went up to the very top where the young eagle was roasting itself in the sun. This man pluckily got his sack and stuffed the bird into it. Down they came step by step and in no time at all they reached the nayvogue. They hopped in and rowed hard and fast until they came to a spot close to the Raven Rock. They then felt that maybe they had made good their escape from the old eagle.

On arrival at Brandon Creek they put the nayvogue up on its stand, went home, tackled the old mule under the cart and reached Dingle in the evening. They met the coastguard who was going to buy the hawk from them and he nearly collapsed on seeing what they had. Instead of giving them four pounds as had been agreed he gave them a pound more. They went into a pub and drowned and baptised the eaglet and themselves too. They didn't go to sea at all the next morning for fear of the old eagle. Perhaps the eaglet's scent might still be in the nayvogue and he would tear both themselves and their nayvogue to pieces.

The eagle returned to the nest after it had been robbed and when he realised that his only chick was missing he went mad. He made for the Island to attack the children and only for all the dogs and the sticks which the islanders had he wouldn't have left a child alive there. He attacked the donkeys and the cows and the sheep. He snatched a calf that was a few months old and carried it up into the air but the calf was too heavy and was weighing him down into the sea with the result that he had to release his grip and the poor calf was drowned. The eagle's rage lasted for two or three days and every living person on the Island feared that he wouldn't leave a child or a woman there. However the fiercest rage is the quickest to abate and so it was with the eagle. He took his leave of the Island and no eagle has ever since been seen there.

People say that this world keeps turning round and round without ever stopping and in due course one of the 'cats' married into the house of a woman in the parish of Dunquin, and proved to be the most marvellous man ever to come into the parish, a fisherman and a hunter, a knowledgeable man who worked hard, and a real saint. He never boasted about his deeds, and reared a large family who grew into fine strong decent men. Whenever people reminded him of the eagle and of the chick which he stole he would reply: 'Ah, anyone who would do that can't have had much sense. What would we do if the old eagle got a hold of us? There wouldn't be much talk of us today.'

An English gentleman once came to Inishvickillane where he had a nice summer-house. A gentleman wants for nothing, they say, and even if he is out of his mind nobody knows whether or which because he is a gentleman. This man had every sort of fire-arm. A gun for seals and a gun for birds, as the man said. The islanders went to see him and told him of their problem with the *dónall dubh* or raven. All he wanted was the wind of the word and so they brought him over from Inish for a day.

At this particular time the raven was hatching and scarcely ever left the nest unless driven to do so by hunger. They brought the Englishman to where the raven was hatching and I'm afraid the hatching was soon over. The raven got a bullet and a second bullet that brought his life to a harsh end. Our friend walked all around the Island that day and killed a half-dozen ravens. 'Life was never like this,' said one man when he saw the gun and the bullet and the slaughter. The grey crow and the kestrel and every other bird that did any damage got the same treatment, and that gun rid the Island of those wild birds as effectively as the swell rids the strand of sand. Many years later the raven used to pay a hurried visit but that was all as he was well aware that, since he had no nest and there were no other ravens around, his enemy was on the lookout. It is said that the birds of the air have their own sense.

After those big birds had been wiped out it wasn't many years until the sea-birds increased greatly in numbers and the islands were chock-full of them. Then the islanders both young and old had grease to their ears from eating sea-birds which were full of oil and fat. That was the time when many people in other places had no appetising food but it was a time of tasty food and fare on the Island.

Inishnabroe is an ideal place for puffins. The rabbits burrow into the ground and as soon as they become aware of the puffin's presence they leave their burrows because should the puffin catch a rabbit in a burrow that was the end of the rabbit, and when it did catch one in the burrow you could hear the screeching in the eastern world. The rabbit would be short-lived because it would die of fright.

The islanders were always prepared for the day of the puffin's arrival, and if the puffins wreaked havoc among the rabbits they themselves suffered the same fate at the hands of the islanders who would spend two days and a night killing them so that when the men arrived home laden with birds the women's fingers had plenty to do plucking them, storing the feathers, cutting them up and curing them. Every house had at least a couple of barrelfuls and those houses which had help had four or five. Such houses weren't short of tasty food.

The birds would leave and not return again for a week until the egg-laying season came but as soon as ever they arrived they began to be hunted. The islanders realised full well that they had laid and so would be confined all the more to the nests. There was a market for the feathers whether the price was high or low. They always brought in a few shillings and the shillings were scarce enough but in spite of all the killing and hunting one would never guess that as much as one of them had been killed.

The puffin is a dangerous bird. He has a pointed beak and if he got to stick it in you he would leave you marked for life. There was a man on the Island who was pricked in the thumb by a puffin and the thumb was sore for a year and a day. When it healed it had the shape of a puffin's beak and retained that shape until the day he died. The steward warned the islanders to stop killing the puffins or else they would suffer for it but they paid little heed to his word of warning and continued to hunt those sea-birds which provided great food and helped to pay the rent.

There were other sea-birds twice as big as the puffin. They were known as guillemots and razor-bills. Because of their size they abounded in feathers and were much sought after by the islanders. Those birds never landed on dry ground. They made their nests, if you could describe them as such, on the rocks in the cliffs, and laid their eggs on the hard rock with neither a wisp of hay nor a rib of hair around them.

Killing them was a dangerous occupation. Three or four men would have to work together using one good long stout rope and another fairly light rope, as well as a stick with a snare attached. The birds might be a couple of hundred feet down the cliff-face. You put one end of the rope around your body and two men held you. You held the snare-stick in your hand and paid the other rope down ahead of you with a bag attached to the end of it. The man on the rope had to be a real expert at the job. As he made his way down he had to remove or throw down the stones which he felt were loose as they were dangerous should they hit the rope around his body. He went down as far as the nests, put his snare-stick to work, pulled out bird after bird and twisted their necks. As he killed them he put them into the bag and the two men on the cliff-top hauled them up. They then emptied the bag and lowered it again.

Only a very brave man would go on the rope but there were tricksters and rascals amongst the islanders too. They pretended that they couldn't bear even to look down the cliff never mind going down. That plan worked for a while so that they didn't have to go to any trouble other than bring the catch home. When the men returned their wives would ask them: 'Who was on the rope today?'

'Myself, upon my soul!' Question followed question but the same poor sucker was on the rope every day.

The women whose husbands were on the rope every day fought a hard battle using their sharp tongues and curses. They warned their husbands not to go down the rope anymore except when their turn came. The skipper of the boat got a bit of a tongue-lashing from those women with the result that he had to agree not to take any man on board who was not prepared to spend a day on the rope. The smart fellows heard about the conversation and the row which the poor suckers' wives kicked up and they didn't like it. They knew that a blow had been struck and they themselves would suffer the consequences. When the hag is hard-pressed she has to make a run for it.

Plucking those birds and then washing and cleaning and salting them was no easy task. They were full of feathers and the islanders made a nice penny out of them. Most of the feathers and the cured birds also were purchased by the people on the mainland. Those cured birds made ten shillings a dozen and any time you are rewarded for your labour you don't hesitate to go down the cliff again. Where there's a will there's a way. Those known as tricksters came to be known as rogues instead because when put to the test they were among the bravest. The new name stuck to them while they lived and to some of their descendants after them.

The islanders always spent the three months of April, May and June hunting those sea-birds, and at the beginning of August they turned their attentions to the puffins. They say that there is no nicer bird to eat than the puffin it is so appetising. When the puffin season came around the steward Bess Rice always arrived with her salt and her firkins to kill them for her. She would dispatch one man from each house to the Tearaght, a sea-rock which teemed with those puffins. Bess was the object of much cursing and swearing but instead of that doing her any harm it only worked to her advantage. However when the islanders had filled the firkins they would give the signal and Bess' boat would go to fetch them. But she was contending with able dealers because they didn't kill the big puffins they came across. Instead they brought them home after her boat had left.

All this work came to an end before the first of August. As soon as the first breeze blew that day the young birds and their mothers would be swimming on the water, but a week later there wouldn't be trace or tidings of them. For them the season was over and they left for the place they had come from and where their instinct led them to return.

The first people to go to live on the Island hunted those birds more than anybody else and used to go as far as Skellig Rock for chicks or young gannets. They too are wonderful birds but very rarely did the islanders succeed in catching them because their habitat was too far away across a very dangerous sea. The generation born on the Island wasn't as hardy or as experienced as their fathers before them. As well as that they were becoming lazy. It was easier to cast a seine-net than to risk being killed by a rock falling from a cliff which might hit you on the top of the head and deprive you of your senses for the rest of the year. That often happened and both the man hit by the stone and the man who saw him being hit were in no mind to go down that cliff again and so that sort of cliff-work came to an end.

The down from these sea-birds is ideal for filling mattresses, and so plentiful was it on the Island that some of the mainland women used to send their newly-made mattresses in to be filled because they themselves had only straw mattresses. It is said also that the mainland women were not at all slow to marry an islandman knowing that they would have a fine soft bed under their backsides at night.

The islanders knocked great value out of seals and hunted them during November. You have to be very skilled in the work before being allowed to go killing them. You would need a beam with four corners on it which narrows back to where you grip it, about three feet long and up to seven pounds in weight. If you fail to hit the seal and knock him out at the first attempt you had better be careful. Quite often it happened that the first blow was not successful nor indeed the second one. Unless you hit him outside the two eyes your blows to any other part of him will have no effect. Frequently the assistance of a second man was required because the seal's belly was turned up as often as his back. That second man might succeed in hitting him a wallop around the nose and so turn him feet up, that is if one could describe his paws as feet.

A day spent killing seals, tying them with ropes, hauling them out of the hole where they are killed, lifting them in over the gunwale of the boat and arranging them in it is a trying arduous day indeed. Some of them were about four hundred-weight. The islanders were mainly interested in the large seals because they contained a large amount of fat and flesh, if indeed it is flesh. Anyone who had a cured seal or two had sufficient food for the spring and light for the winter. The fat of the seal was rich in oil and was tasty when salted because it wasn't of itself too salty due to the oil.

The fat was cut off the black meat because that fat contained all the oil, or *úsc* as it was called. You cut the fat into small pieces, put those pieces into a fairly large pot and left them on the fire for most of the day. When it was well-done it turned red in colour. That indicated that all the fat had been removed. The pot was then taken outdoors and when it cooled the oil was put into earthen jars which would keep it in good condition for years. The boiled fat remaining in the pot after the oil had been removed was put into a wooden box and was excellent for lighting fires.

The islanders' light consisted of a cresset and oil from the seal. The cresset was a piece of a metal pot or oven on two sticks stuck into the wall. You poured the oil into it and put the wick into the oil. Thick rushes made the ideal wick. The rushes which had to be peeled would provide the best part of a week's light before finally giving out. There were always three or four rushes in every cresset and the light was just like the Dingle train belching steam and smoke as it arrived at the station. That didn't worry the islanders. They knew no different and were content as could be sitting under the cresset as it provided them with light.

The seal was their source of light, fire and food, and they were thankful to God who provided them with it.

4

The first people to inhabit the Island didn't have any boats because the boats in those days were too big and too heavy and there was no proper landing-place where they could keep them safely or haul them up out of the water. Their relatives on the mainland helped them out because all of the islanders' time was taken up with herding. They did little fishing other than from the rocks because they had no knowledge of nets or lobster-pots or spillers. Their year was divided into four seasons, from Christmas to St Patrick's Day, from St Patrick's Day to St John's Day (24 June), from St John's Day until Michaelmas (29 September) and from Michaelmas to Christmas.

The second generation of islanders were becoming wiser and wished to have boats of their own. They requested the land-agent to provide them with a landing-place and he didn't fail them. He sent workmen into the Island and a small slip was built there. The large rocks were blasted into the air and room was made for boats to land. That slip is still there today. First one boat came and then a second, both of them large with eight men in each. They were doing well but the little pier provided room for only a few boats and those people who brought in the first boats had legal right to the place. There was a fine cove slightly to the west of the houses and people who later acquired boats made an anchorage there and used to moor them in that place both in winter and in summer. Ever since it has been known as the Boat Cove.

Those boats made seine-fishing possible. The islanders quickly learned the art and set to work fishing because at that time fish were as plentiful around the Island as the sand on the strand. It was nothing but salt and barrels and cured fish from one end of the year to the other. They had fish to eat going to bed and again as soon as they put their foot out of bed in the morning. They brought fish to Dingle twice a month, and the moment the boat reached the slip there the hucksters would arrive and buy every single fish in the boats. There was no mention of steak or rashers in those days and most people had no idea as to what they were. 'Any bit of fish boiled?' was the question the housewife was always asked.

The third generation of islanders were the ones who began fishing for mackerel and lobsters – that was well into the end of the nineteenth century. Gradually the big boats ceased to be used because they were too heavy and too cumbersome, and anyhow the islanders were becoming wiser and wiser.

The first nayvogue that ever came to the Western Island came up, we are told, from Farran, a grassy place below the Connor Pass. A man named Hartney is reputed to have built it and to have come to Farran from County Clare. It is said that the day the nayvogue was built it cost only three pounds including the cost of the carrier and his horse. The two who purchased it brought it from the pier in Dingle west through Dingle Bay to the Island pier although they had little experience of such a craft. However they didn't take long to master it. When the people on the Island saw the nayvogue approaching the pier all the women and children were screaming that the men on board were close to drowning, that they wouldn't be able to get out of it and so would die on board. They had never before laid eyes on anything like it.

The nayvogue came into the pier and both men and oars were taken off. Those on the slip were amazed when they saw two half-bags of flour, two hundred-weight of salt and many other goods on board also. The old ways were disappearing and being replaced by new ones. The arrival of the nayvogue brought happiness and delight and relief to the Island if for no other reason, as the man said, than that it put an end to the *collachs* which was the name they gave the large boats.

Manxmen and Arklow fishermen arrived with their large vessels to fish for May mackerel. They used nets and fished by night and showed the islanders how to fish for mackerel. They also told them where they could come by nets suitable for nayvogues. That is almost a hundred years ago if not more.

Life on the Island was beginning to prosper just at the time the nayvogue arrived. They used it to fish for mackerel and lobsters and were really delighted with it. Mackerel-fishing went on throughout the year in those times because they were very plentiful. The islanders used to go out fishing every fine night that came. There was a crew of three in each nayvogue and they could both launch it and take it out of the water without any difficulty. Some of them often remarked that it was God who sent it their way the very first day.

The Manxmen came in a few large vessels and anchored in Ventry Harbour. They always salted all their catch. As soon as their boats were full they headed out the harbour and across to England where a market for the fish awaited them. That journey used to take quite a while as the boats did not have engines. They were dependent on sail and wind which meant that during the summer they were often too long at sea with the result that the fish sometimes went bad and they were obliged to dump it back into the sea. The first hundreds of May mackerel which the islanders caught and sold to those boats in Ventry Harbour fetched five pounds a hundred. That amazed the islanders and almost caused them to lose their heads.

If the sea was calm the lobster-fishing began in March and continued to the end of August. An Englishman was the first person ever to put a lobster-pot in the sea off the Western Island, and after catching nine or ten dozen lobsters he used to take them to Cahirciveen and send them by train to Dublin and from there to England where they made good money. However the islanders soon learned the business from him and made their own pots modelled on those used by him. They got going immediately with each man doing the work of two, as the old man said. They were getting five and six shillings a dozen, great money at that time. There was no expense involved. It was just a matter of taking them out of the pots.

Large boats began coming to buy the lobsters from the islanders. Each boat had a large tank with salt-water running through it and in that tank they kept the lobsters which they brought from the islanders. When full it held four hundred dozen. Because these boats had no engines it used to take them a long time to bring the cargo to England, unless of course they had a good fresh wind behind them. If they had they would go over there and back within ten days. When they returned there was always a large catch of lobsters waiting for them.

There was no question of the islanders fixing a price. The English always fixed their own price but the islanders didn't care as long as the English bought the lobsters. Nobody else was interested in buying them. The English brought great relief to the islanders who knew they had no alternative if the English failed them, which they didn't.

That first nayvogue that came to the Island was called the *Beauty*. It won a race in Ventry Harbour once and the poet Ó Duinnshléibhe who was a fearless mocker composed a lovely poem about it and its crew. That poem remained on people's tongues until very recently. The *Beauty* won wide acclaim and before long a son of Hartney's came to this area and began making nayvogues. A man here and there learned the trade and soon three men were working full time at it because demand was firm and many fellows were going to sea. As the old people used to say, 'fish and gold and money, plenty of porter and red whiskey'. This great boom, the gold factory as they called it, occurred back at the end of the nineteenth century. Fishing was in its prime because the mackerel were being cured locally. There was a curing-shed in Murreagh, another in Ballydavid, a third in Bealbawn and a fourth in Dunquin. That was the time when a man remarked in a pub that there were far more fish-fins in his wife's hands that in his own although she had never been to sea.

Any man who could even stand had a pound and a shilling in his pocket in those days. There is no telling the amount of money made by shrewd people who along with their grown-up sons were able to fish. Some of them even purchased large patches of land which are in the possession of their grandchildren to this day.

It is said that a man from Clogher was building nayvogues in that townland at the same time as Hartney was building them down below the hill in Farran, and it is said too that a nayvogue made by him had been brought to the Island before Hartney's one arrived there but no year or date is mentioned regarding either of them. The man from Clogher was known to the islanders as Dónall Ó Catháin of the Nayvogues and two brothers of the O'Sullivan family brought the first ever of his nayvogues to the Island. Another Ó Catháin man from Clogher also built nayvogues and he was known as Tomás Dhónaill Óig. I cannot say if he was a son of Dónall of the Nayvogues or not. Tradition has it that the Ó Catháins first came to the Island from Graigue and from Clogher, which would mean that they were connected, as indeed the Ó Catháin's on the mainland and those on the Island were and still are. The mother of the present writer was an Ó Catháin who was born and bred on the Island.

There was another gifted man by the name of Ó Cíobháin – he was known as the Tommy Tiúithí – who lived in Glanlick in the parish of Dunquin. People said that he too built nayvogues. Whenever a new nayvogue came to the Island they used to say: 'Indeed it will be all right if it is as good as Tiúithí's.' It seems therefore that Ó Cíobháin was a good hand at making the mould because it has always been said that it is the mould that makes the good nayvogue.

An Ó Dálaigh man from the Island learned how to make the mould and began to build nayvogues for himself whenever he required one. Another man then came and learned from Ó Dálaigh. He too used to build a nayvogue whenever he needed one. Ó Súilleabháin came after those two. He still builds nayvogues but it is Ó Dálaigh's son Tomás who now builds them for anyone who asks him to do so. He it was who built the nayvogue which made the journey around Ireland.*

Though nayvogues were once numerous and highly regarded they are now becoming extinct and for every hundred in the Dingle Peninsula twenty years ago there is only one today. Just as the nayvogue replaced the big boat so too has it been replaced itself by engine-driven boats, and the nayvogue is no more lamented than were the big boats.

Life is comfortable for the present day fisherman. The young fishermen you meet nowadays say that those who preceded them were just sea-horses forever rowing through gales of winds and foaming seas. I agree. All one has to do now is throw the lobster-pot out of the boat and the engine will haul it up from the sea-bed. Signs on each of those boats carries a couple of hundred pots, the work is light and the financial return for their toil is good. They have cooking facilities if they need them and there is no shortage of tea.

For a time after the arrival of the 'pledge-priest' here any night the islanders went fishing the nets would be full of dogfish from bottom to cork and those dogfish would make ribbons of the nets which might or might not contain fish. The nets which used to be anchored in the harbour could not be taken on board the nayvogue because of the weight of the dogfish. The poor fishermen whose livelihood was destroyed by them kicked up hullabaloo.

'Ye wouldn't be in that situation, ye pack of devils,' said Pilib, 'if ye had kept the pledge. See now what ye have gained from it? Nothing but death from hunger and misery.'

Of course Pilib himself never kept the pledge for two successive days. All he wanted was to start an argument.

Necessity they say is the mother of invention and ideas come as a result of good advice. Two men went around the parish looking for money with a view to offering sacrifice to God so that the dogfish would be banished from the place. They called to the parish priest and informed him in detail why they had come. He listened kindly to them and said that he would indeed offer sacrifice to God so that the sea around them be cleared of the dogfish, but he told them: 'Ye too must pray to God for relief.'

The next time they went mackerel-fishing the man on the bottom of the net hauled in the first section and what was in it? Two dogfish, each with a mackerel in its mouth! 'It's the same god-damned story again tonight,' he said to the crew. They became despondent but when he hauled in more of the net there were mackerel in it but no dogfish. Nobody said a word until the last of the nets was on board. They contained a couple of thousand mackerel and just the two dogfish. Each man took off his cap and praised and thanked the God of Glory and his power. They knew all about moon miracles and soon they realised that God had a hand in the work.

The fishing flourished from then on but the dogfish were completely wiped out. The fishermen continued offering sacrifice year in year out and gladly paid for it. They also implored God to keep them free from the dogfish. Indeed the dogfish were never afterwards as plentiful on the sea-surface nor did they damage any nets. They are still plentiful on the sea-bed but don't come to the surface as they used to do.

A great amount of timber was recovered from the sea prior to the beginning of this century, because at that time large sailing-ships used to carry timber from country to country and they suffered badly from bad weather. Gales of wind and spring tides used to throw them on to the rocks which made matchwood of their hulls and scattered their cargoes of timber all over the sea. The islanders were delighted to see that happening provided, of course, the crew survived. They believed that it was God who sent it their way. They would go out in their nayvogues and bring in hundreds of boards ranging from twelve to twenty feet in length. There were big long baulks of red deal thirty feet in length and a couple of feet square. They would tie those boards and beams with a rope, tow them after the nayvogue and un-load them on the White Strand at full tide. When a board or baulk is hauled a certain distance up on that strand it stays there. Every part of the island where timber could be landed was chock-full of it. People would come in from the mainland and buy what-ever amount they required. It was cheap at the price but dear enough in fact for those buying it because they were of limited means.

The islanders set about repairing their houses and adding an extra room or two. Why wouldn't they? Wasn't the timber itself free and weren't they themselves well able to put it to good use? Only felt and nails needed to be bought and since they had a lot of spare timber to sell the additions to their houses cost them nothing. In this way the old hovels on the Island were improved a little without state or government aid. The govern-ment across the water ran this country but the islanders in those days knew nothing about government or state. All they wished for was to live an honest and peaceful life and have enough to eat. They had in fact plenty to eat, Danish pigs' heads and sides, pigs' feet that were eighteen inches long and fine fat rabbits. Nobody came to claim the wrack even if all the islands were full of it.

One particular day a man spotted a sheep and a lamb on a large clod of earth on a cliff-ledge. He returned home and told his story. Four men quickly got together with ropes and a stick suitable for use with a snare and they set out. They first attempt-ed to snare the lamb but if they did it fell and landed on the rocky beach below but wasn't killed. Then they turned their attentions to the sheep, succeeded quickly in snaring her and brought her to the cliff-top. They then brought her to the spot above where the lamb was lying but the lamb was unable to climb up as the cliff was too high. Three of them had to go down, corner the lamb under a projecting rock and catch it.

Everything was grand. They sat down and had a smoke. Whatever glance one of them gave in under the rock what should he see there but a long narrow object resembling a bolt, approximately two feet long and gold in colour. One of the others on seeing the bolt agreed that it was copper. The lamb was brought up to the sheep and both were let off out the hill. The men immediately went back down and in no time at all they had gathered their load of copper in under the large rocks. They put it up on their backs and brought it home as fast as their legs could carry them. Then they returned for more and along with them went every man who was capable of descending the cliff, each with his own bag. They continued collecting the copper for quite a good while until the very last bolt was recovered. There were many other rocky beaches around the Island but little copper was found on them. People say that a storm had carried a *cleith* or large part of a wrecked ship in there many years previously – there is a heavy swell there at all times of the year – and that as soon as the *cleith* came in it was smashed to bits. Ever since that beach has been known as the Copper Beach.

So far so good. The islanders gained no benefit from the copper. Some of them had a large amount of it while others had little as happens with all things in life. It is said that drunkenness cannot keep a secret and sometimes when an islander was over on the mainland he might let the cat out of the bag, particularly if he was in the way of getting drink. The blue-uniformed coast-guards in Dunquin in those days were on the look-out for wreckage around the coast. They got the whiff of the copper as a result of people's talk but weren't really certain as to who had it. You can rest assured that they were keeping a close eye out for it but it was easy to find a place on the Island where the copper could be hidden.

The islanders had the copper but hadn't yet found a buyer. However a fellow who has a ship and cargo will be favoured by the wind some day. The blue-uniformed men came to the Island one day in the hope of coming upon some of the copper or finding some stupid islander who would confirm that the copper was in fact there. They spoke only English but the islanders sang dumb because they hated the sight of them coming.

There was a shopkeeper in Dingle, a local man who had spent twenty years before the mast as a coast-guard in the British navy. He had returned home on pension and settled down in Dingle. He bought and sold everything and anything. He got a tip-off from someone or other that the islanders had the copper so he sent them word to bring it along and he would reward them well. On hearing this the islanders suspected that some kind of a trap was being set for them because that man had spent his life in the British navy and was a coast-guard at one stage. They feared that he had now been chosen to catch them out. Everyday he would send a message asking why they weren't bringing the copper along.

The best thing to do was to call to see him. A boat went from the Island to Dingle one fine day and there was a man on board who had two bags of wool. The man who wanted the copper bought wool as well as everything else and when the boat reached the pier in Dingle he was there waiting. He asked for the wool and if he did he wasn't refused. The islander was as happy as a child with a couple of sweets.

'Listen here to me,' he said to the buyer, 'it is like this,' telling him that there were two or three copper bolts in the bag, but that he wasn't to weigh them until the others had left the shop. The buyer was delighted and gave the islanders a good jorum of drink.

When it was getting late into the evening the islanders were collecting their chattels to put them on board. Most of their goods were in this man's shop. When everything was in order he said: 'I'll now give ye a drink for the road.' He went behind the counter and poured out a half-glass of whiskey and a pint of porter for each man.

'Here,' he said, 'drink my health and the health of the good men present.'

They praised him to the skies saying that he was the best man ever put on earth by God, yet because they didn't know him sufficiently well they didn't altogether trust him. They were still between two minds about him. The man inside put his hand under the counter and took out a copper bolt about two feet long.

38

'Whisper,' he said, 'is that bolt the same as the ones ye've got?'

The men nearly collapsed when shown a bolt exactly like their own. They couldn't utter a word. They were really dumbfounded.

'That is one of yeer bolts,' he said, 'and don't be so afraid of me because even if I did spend most of my life in John Bull's navy it wasn't because of love for it or enjoyment. Bring me the copper,' he said, 'and I'll reward ye. But,' he said, 'beware of the coast-guards in Ballykeen. I imagine that they are not too strict or too loyal to the queen but a man has to make a living somehow.'

His words reassured the islanders because they saw that they made sense and so they agreed that if coming to Dingle they would bring a load of bolts. He warned them to bring only a few at a time for fear they might raise the suspicions of the coast-guards who were also in Dingle at the time. The bargain was struck and one of the men piped up: 'Fair dues to you,' he said, 'and aren't you the true brother of Judas?'

They arrived home safe and sound together with their chattels. Those who had the copper decided to sell some of the bolts to the man in Dingle as they had no hope of getting anything for them from anybody else. They set out a week later having collected some rabbit-skins and a few half-bags of wool with the bolts wrapped inside, and off they went east through Dingle Bay never stopping until the prow of the boat reached Máire Lyne's slip in Dingle Harbour. One of the men leaped ashore, went up to the shopkeeper and told him to move fast. No sooner said than done. The shopkeeper dispatched his horse and cart back to the pier and removed everything from the boat.

The business was completed and they were at ease. A cloud of smoke was reaching up to the sun from every pipe. Then this coast-guard came over and began to talk to them. That is all the good it did him, however, as he spoke only English and they spoke only Irish. He went away just as he had come. They were too smart for him. They tied up the boat as did the old warriors long ago even if they were going to be away for only an hour. They didn't all enter the shop together but waited for a lull for fear they were being watched from behind a fence. Everything went fine. They got quite a lot of money from the shopkeeper.

That was unusual as they had rarely got either gold or silver from any merchants in Dingle except for whatever few pence those merchants might pull out from the bottom of their pockets. The Dingle man bought all the bolts they had collected and would have bought more if they had them, and he said that the profit that he had made from those bars was the easiest money he had ever made. Coming home in the boat Pilib spoke.

'Sure only for me wouldn't those bolts have rotted? The brave man never lost it,' said he.

Early one morning a man went to the door and looked out to sea. He saw a black-backed gull standing on a large black mound and knew that there was something worthwhile under its feet. He called the man next door and the man next to him again and they headed in the direction of the mound. What was it but a great big bullock of up to ten hundred-weight! They put a rope around his neck and hauled him up on the pier which was not too far away. They left him tied there until such time as the tide receded so that they could skin him at their ease. When the tide receded leaving them room to work they brought along all the necessary equipment – knives each of which would cut a rib of hair off your head and hatchets which would sink in six inches at every stroke – and in no time at all they had skinned him. He was then turned belly-up to remove his intestines but the moment the knife was stuck into him out came the poison and the smell was so awful that it almost killed the weak ones amongst them. Some of them said that he was rotten and that they had better stay clear of him in case he might be worse than even the yellow oil. But alas and alack, as the women said, the only pity was that he wasn't bigger whatever about the smell. What the islanders needed most was meat and now they had it under their feet.

Panniers were brought from every house in the village and it didn't take long to remove the bullock from the slip. A barrel and salt were provided and the meat was washed three times and then salted. There was plenty of tasty beef for six months. As the man from Dunquin said, there was hair on the chest of every islandman just like a bull. Every man, woman and child had grease to their ears while the bullock lasted.

During the year of the bullock two islandwomen gave birth to twins. Those four children, three boys and a girl, grew up strong and were christened 'the bullock's family'.

5

The first people to inhabit the Western Island brought a great gift with them, the living faith which they had inherited from previous generations. That living faith was acquired not from reading books but from their fathers and mothers who day and night taught it by their words and talk and prayers, and what they taught lasted as long as people lived on the Island. Every person born and reared on the Island who is still alive, wherever in the world he or she is, has that living faith in his heart and will not abandon it until death. It has always been said that what enters one's heart never leaves it. The faith which you learn by your own fireside is the faith you will follow all through your life. No matter what you say or do the faith you have from the cradle is in your blood and you cannot part with it. If you do something wrong you will soon realise it because it will cause your mind to be worried and you won't be happy until you receive pardon for that evil deed, that is if it does affect you. Perhaps there are people who act as they please but there are two sides to that page, the side of faith and the other side, that of prudence and sense.

There never was and never will there be a fisherman without faith. Fishermen spent their lives under God's weather, and they were often at death's door but were saved by the grace of God. Whatever faith you profess it is strong when you are at sea because the sea has neither pity nor mercy for anyone. Even the French sailors who frequent this coast have the strongest faith of all. If you happened to board their boats you would see the signs of their living faith. The cabin where they eat and drink and the bunks in which they sleep are full of pictures of their native country's saints and of printed prayers with frames and glass on them. Naturally those prayers are all in French, their own native language. That is my reason for saying that the living faith will remain with fishermen until their dying day. I and others in my situation have ample proof of that.

Islands are places where, if the inhabitants have any prayer at all in their heads or hearts, their faith will be strengthened and deepened as a result of the signs they see coming from God. It is

42

better to witness one portent than to be listening to people chattering all your life. The portent goes to one's heart but talk is slow to impress. The islanders had a great interest in the sun in the morning and the moon at night. Many was the prayer and petition made to God because of them, praising and thanking him for his gifts, his great power and his goodness to them, They offered up in sacrifice to him whatever stress or trouble came their way and they always accepted both good and bad from the Almighty. Each of them was full of the living faith. Perhaps an odd one might let on to have doubts but that was only on the outside, as the man said. If your faith is weak you can't stand up to much.

The faith of the people now dead for many years was far stronger than that of the old people today, not to mind the young ones. Some of them used to say that nobody could exist on prayers, that only simple people prayed, that they had spoilt the young people and were themselves becoming simple-minded from too much praying. God and Mary be with us, the real confusion came with the bad times, the poverty when there were no potatoes or meal. It would take a staunch person not to be confused by that. It did indeed confuse them, not because of a lack of faith, because the person who is hungry will stop at nothing. People in those days held that it was no harm if a person accepted food from whatever source, and that is what the smart ones did.

It is said that the Ferriters who lived on the Island seven hundred and fifty years ago were Catholics, but the world is said to change every twenty years, and anyone who is advanced in years can see clear evidence of that. He has only to go back to the days of the soup. That memory has not been clouded by the years and clear traces of it still remain on the Island as in every other part of Ireland.

There were two schools on the Island at that time. The instruction given in both wasn't the same. They differed greatly. Nobody ever thought of setting up a national school there until the readers of the *Speckled Cat** arrived, set up their own school and were happy to teach all who wished to attend. English and Irish were taught in that school, whereas in the 'right school', as the Catholic school was called, only English was taught because

43

the government who owned it wished to wipe out the islanders' native language as quickly as possible.

That was impossible and it proved so. The instruction was not the only good thing about the *Speckled Cat* school. There was also the fine food and the soup and the yellow meal which the master used to give the scholars. That school was trying to entice and rebaptise the unfortunate people who didn't realise what they were doing, and because they didn't realise it they joined up. I imagine they wouldn't join only for the fact that their stomachs were empty. The Irish language was the best and most effective instrument to bring that about.

The children attending the 'right school' got nothing but trouncing with the cane, and were weak from cold and hunger and other such hardships. Yet in spite of the soup and the meal and the importance attached to the Irish language not many of the Island's children attended the other school. The teacher taught his own religion there, fathers and mothers found out what he was up to, and they objected strongly. The whole effort fell through and the game was up even though a great deal of money had been spent on it.

There are two sides to every story and you shouldn't believe either without first hearing the other. Then one can judge according as one wishes. Wasn't life very very hard on a mother and father and children weak from hunger without food or sustenance or any great likelihood of getting any? When the old hag is hard-pressed she has to make a run for it. Like the man on board a ship which is in flames on the high seas, when the heat and the flames reach him his only option to avoid being burned is to leap into the water. Death from hunger is another kind of death, and a fine natural one compared to being burned alive. The islanders were struggling on as best they could but, alas, they could no longer maintain the fight against hunger and had to yield and put something into their stomachs or else lie down and allow themselves and their families to die of starvation, and that would make no sense at all.

There was a priest in the Dingle Peninsula about a hundred years ago, a very learned man. He had the faith and was doing his best trying to tend his flock but his faith weakened, he abandoned it and converted to that of the minister. He also married

44

the minister's daughter. Nobody else followed his example, however, which shows that he had lost his senses and could not help it any more than the woman who goes to the strand and drowns herself. If she does so not many women follow her example. Such actions show a lack of reason. The priest's action caused commotion and comment. That was the period when the priests and people of the right faith, as one might say, were under pressure and the grey-clothed ministers came out boasting about it. That is all the good it did them, however. The ministers and the unfortunate priest disappeared. The poor islanders are still with us and still have a living faith, thank God, and there is neither trace nor tidings of any minister on this side of Tralee.

While life was reasonably good there was little talk of priests or ministers. There never was nor is there today nor will there be any mention of them as long as people have sufficient to eat and drink. The ordinary person doesn't spend his life talking about religion. He finds it difficult enough to go to God's House one day a week and thinks that the time that Mass takes is longer than the longest season of the year. You would see some people outside the church door sending clouds of tobacco smoke up in the air while the Offering is taking place inside. That is certainly not a nice example from fathers of families, but in fact that often occurred and still does, if I may say so.

The priest endeavoured to stop such conduct by speaking reasonably at Mass and even going outside a few times when only halfway through Mass, but instead of entering the church those people used to leap over the fences and remain there until Mass was over. When a reasonable priest who has people of that type under his care gives sound advice and is not listened to there is nothing he can do other than give them all the rope they want and not go running after them. All they wanted was to get the priest to come out but they failed and the day came when some of them were no longer there nor did anyone know where they had gone. That too will be the fate of those who still follow such practices but of course there is no cure for foolishness.

That is life. It is said that you will never find two who are alike. Those who used to remain outside the church door were just as strong in their faith as most of those inside and they knew

45

that the real devils were inside because fear wouldn't allow them to remain outside as they weren't fully free from sin. As those who witnessed these events said, they were acting honestly and they brought no harm to anyone except possibly themselves.

There was once a man on the Island whose faith was as strong as that of any of his likes, but he always did just what suited himself. Being the father of a young family he was short of help and worked from dawn to dusk every day of the week. He had a nice-sized flock of sheep on the hill but never had time to go and check on them except on Sundays. While all the other islanders were preparing to go out to Mass in Dunquin he would be getting ready to go up the hill. Every Sunday he would go on his knees and pray to God, and as soon as the boats had left for Mass he would take his stick, call his dog and head for the hill where he would remain until the boats carrying the islanders were on their way home. For him Sunday was then over and he was happy as a knight. Those islanders who had gone to Mass would on their return prepare a meal and eat it and then go to check on their flock and they had ample time to do so.

Your man's sheep never really prospered. If a black-backed gull was noticed picking at a sheep and a boat went to the spot to check you could be sure that the sheep was one of his. It made no difference. He never changed his ways. He continued every Sunday morning to head for the hill with his stick and his dog while all the neighbours were on their way to Mass. His wife often asked him why he didn't do like everyone else in the village.

'Ah,' he would say, 'they have plenty of help, something which I haven't got and so I must do as I'm doing.'

'Haven't you got your own help growing up,' she would reply, 'and you're not giving them very good example?'

He was a headstrong man but never did his neighbours any harm. In fact he did them many good turns. Whenever he was on the hill he would move his neighbours' sheep out of danger as well as his own. Consequently they were grateful knowing full well that he wasn't out to harm them. He continued on in that manner for quite a while and nobody interfered, but his wife was constantly complaining that he was different from all the other men on the Island in the way he spent Sundays.

One particular Sunday, however, the islanders both young and old went out to Dunquin to hear God's Mass but your man went up the hill with his dog and his stick. When the wind is from the south all the sheep move to the north side of the Island and when the wind is north they go over to the south side. As there was a fresh breeze from the south he went back to the Pass of the Slope convinced that all the sheep would be on the north side after the night. When he put his head over the pass and had a view of the north side not a single sheep was to be seen. He stopped and pondered for a moment. He knew full well that he was the only person at the top of the hill, and where had everyone's sheep gone?

He reddened his pipe, sat down for a while and said to himself that something strange had happened that had never before happened. Having smoked his fill he took up his stick and continued on up the hill towards the south side to see if there were any sheep at all alive on the Island. He quickly crossed over the Gusty Pass because he was convinced that pirates must have stolen them. When he came to a spot where he could see the south side and saw what was before him he nearly passed out with fright. All the sheep on the island had gathered together and were lying down in one spot dead asleep with a big bright beam of light shining on them from a spot some distance up at the bottom of the hill. His legs and hands began to tremble, his stick fell from his grasp and for an hour he had no idea where he was. That was the very time that Mass was being said in Dunquin. When he recovered the sheep had scattered in every direction and were moving around as they pleased. He took off his hat, went down on his knees and thanked the God of Glory for what had happened him.

He returned home in a happier state of mind than on any previous Sunday. Not a word did he utter to any living person, his own wife included. The week passed by and Sunday came as usual at the start of the following week. If it did your man didn't ignore it. He was the first man on the pier on his way to Mass in Dunquin. All eyes were on him but from the way he was dressed everyone knew well that he was going out. They were saying to themselves that something must have occurred which had brought about the change. They were talking away wondering if they could find out what it was but nobody could. A second Sunday came and then a third and as Sunday followed Sunday your man was never missing and he kept up going to Mass for as long as he could tie his shoe-laces.

It is said that drunkenness cannot keep a secret and that is indeed true because a man when drunk doesn't have the same sense as when he is sober. There came a Christmas and the islanders went to Dingle as usual. When they had completed their business and were ready for the road home they dropped into a pub. They wetted the year and the Christmas in style and, as is often said, a hen doesn't cackle in the morning the way she does in the evening. Every man's gizzard was full and they were talking about this and that. Someone asked the man who was short of help if something he had seen had caused him to change his ways.

'Perhaps it wouldn't be right for me,' he said, 'not to say publicly what I saw,' and then he described in detail what had occurred and what he had seen. Not one person said a word while he was speaking. They were all dumbfounded.

They came home from Dingle in good spirits but your man's story and the miracle that had occurred were a source of worry to them, some saying that he had fainted while others believed that he had had a stroke but had shaken off its effects completely while he was in the faint. At the same time the miracle upset them greatly, especially since that fellow who hadn't been to Sunday Mass for many years was ever afterwards the first man on the boat pier every Sunday.

He continued to work away on his own as usual and he was indeed a hard worker. Every Sunday after Mass he went up to the hill just like all the other islanders did, but people tend to forget things after a time, and so it was in his case. All those living on the Island had forgotten the miracle but the nickname 'Miracle' stuck to him until the day he died. Some people were waiting for the day when 'Miracle' would do himself some harm but they in fact came closer to harming themselves, something which they never expected. We are told that he died a holy death in his own home and in his own bed with his family gathered around him.

Instead of weakening the living faith on the Island that miracle only strengthened it. If ever an islandman missed Mass on two or three successive Sundays some of them would say that he should go up to the Gusty Pass and witness the type of miracle your man witnessed. That would get him out good and fast. There must have been something in it because the islanders never did a stroke until after Mass.

The priests used to hold the Stations on the Island once a year, in the summer of course. At Dunquin Mass one of them would request that a boat be out on Dunquin Pier before eight o'clock in the morning. Everybody knew beforehand which crews were to go out for the priests. They were the ones who had the hardest task at Station-time and they would prefer any job to it. These poor unfortunate men would have to do without a taste of food or drink or even a smoke from twelve o'clock the night before, row out three miles of sea in windy weather, and bring the curate and the sacristan to the Island in one nayvogue and the parish priest in another. The crew in each boat consisted of three men. Then they had to row three miles back in. It wasn't too difficult if they had a good fresh wind behind them because they had nice sails on the nayvogues. In summer, however, that rarely occurred.

The priests used to begin hearing confessions as soon as they reached the school where they later said two Masses. They would first hear the schoolchildren's confessions, but that arrangement never found favour with the crews who had brought the priests in nor indeed with the islanders as a whole because it meant too much hardship for the crews who had to go so long without a drink or a smoke. Lack of food didn't worry them but the drink and the smoke, as they used to say, did. Yet nobody ever said a word. The holy priests knew about everything except stress. Of that they had no experience.

One day there was a man on the pier who welcomed them warmly. It fell to the lot of two sons of his who were married on the Island to go out for the priests but when the priests passed him by on their way up to the school he glanced after them.

'Upon my soul, boys,' he said, 'neither yeer fathers nor anybody else made ye do any rowing, and ye won't have any great lumps on yeer hands when yeer life's work is over.'

The Stations continued for many years and the islanders were delighted as one year followed another. Why wouldn't they? Had they not received the year's extreme unction and penance and, as the old man remarked about himself, his slate was clean again for another year. There were people on the Island in those days also who feared neither God nor man. They would give free rein to their tongue and the priests didn't always escape its lash.

A curate was once appointed to the parish of Ballyferriter. The islanders knew his people well but didn't know himself. Those who know your origins know yourself, and so it was in this priest's case, even if he never inherited his people's qualities. His Irish was better than both his Latin and his English since his parents had only Irish, the language which he got from the cradle. The language you have from your childhood is the one you will really master and if ever there was a priest in Ireland who had a mastery of Irish it was this young priest. Even if he didn't write any poetry he composed a good deal of it because he spoke the language poetically.

Pilib heard that he had arrived and if he did he found no fault with the young man as a priest.

'O God of Glory,' he said, 'wasn't it enough to have your father down on top of our heads without having his son on our doorstep every day of our lives?'

Philip was at the Stations on the Island one day and who should be collecting the money only this curate! When Pilib came out someone asked him how the man inside was conducting himself.

'He's carrying on just as he saw his father doing. Breeding will always show itself.'

The next man to come out was asked about the young priest.

'His only fault is that he has too much Irish and grumbling will do you no good. He knows every damned thing that happened since the time they sold the copper to his father.'

Time passed and the young priest proved both spirited and shrewd. He was well equipped for his task and knew all there was to be known about the people of the locality. There wasn't a man, woman, child or old person who wasn't fond of him because he always spoke Irish. Life, however, doesn't always turn out as we would wish and perhaps a change is better than no change. The day came when the copper priest had to gather up his belongings and go elsewhere.

The people of Letteragh spoke only Irish when this priest was young. There were many old men and old women who couldn't speak as much as a word of English and so somebody had to come to their aid. That fell to your man's lot and so he had to go down over the hill to them. When leaving Ballyferriter he said a few words in each church and expressed his thanks to his parishioners.

'All I have gained from my Irish,' he said, 'is that I'm being transferred to one of the worst parishes in Ireland.'

He was well aware that Letteragh consisted only of mountain, heather and furze.

The Islanders weren't very sorry at his departure, not because of his personality but because his father knew too much about them just as they did about his father.

It is said that everything is only a nine days' wonder and so it was with the poor curate. A strapping young priest replaced him in Ballyferriter. He wasn't as fluent in Irish as the previous man, a fact which didn't worry him as long as he was able to fulfil his duties. He wasn't long 'grazing' in the area before the people noticed that he wasn't at all keen on drink or drinking. They felt that he was hell-bent against it and would cause havoc if allowed to remain in the place. As the man said when the curate was leaving the area, his going made no difference now because he had destroyed the place forever more.

This new priest turned his attention to drink and to giving the pledge to both young and old. He spared nobody no matter what their disease or complaint. He would start roaring just like a bull out on Beginis would do when eyeing the cattle on the Island, knowing that he couldn't swim in to them. The poor simple people were shaking in their shoes and were terrified of him. It was said that no bailiff ever set foot on the Island who was worse than he was. There was an old saying, however, about landlords and stewards. There was never a landlord or steward of any kind about whom the people had a good word to say, and that is when the old saying was aired: 'There was a bell in the church which didn't have a sweet tone, but then there came another bell which by comparison made the first one sound sweet-toned.'

That is how it was with the landlords and stewards. The man who came was always seven times worse than the man who had left. When people saw what the pledge priest was up to they were high in their praise of the copper priest. No wonder the church-bell cropped up in conversation. This new priest rid the Island of the drink known as the Bandon Rattler and nearly caused the death of the old couple who sold it, so terrified and scared were they. I can assure you that life on the Island had changed by then, the people were somewhat confused and some of them were very nearly out of their minds. The priest just stopped short of clinging to the ground anyone who refused to take the pledge from him.

That situation persisted for a good while, but upon my soul it didn't last forever at all. Pilib who by this time was home from America for many years had no love for the priests who were so hard on the poor people struggling valiantly with life, often with little means and very often with none at all. Pilib spoke out. The islanders were on his side but didn't pretend to be for fear of the priest. He was really out of his mind, as the people said, but he didn't realise it. There wasn't a person in the parish who didn't take the pledge except for some of them who went on the run and whom he failed to catch up with.

Naturally pub-owners were not happy with matters as they stood. They had paid for drink licences but nobody was drinking. The people hardest hit by the pledge were the poor fishermen who spent each night out at sea and a good stretch of the following morning preparing the fish for sale. However it is said that there is a short-cut to the solution of every problem. The islanders got in a stock of bottles of whiskey and hid them underground. On returning home after a night's fishing they would take a swig out of the bottle and it was no small swig. They had taken the words of the pledge but, as they said, a pledge administered by force doesn't last nor indeed does anything else which is forced upon you against your will. This intrigue was taking place not only on the Island but throughout the whole area and never was as much drink consumed as during the time it was banned.

Porter was a thing of the past on the Island because the priest unjustly cursed the innocent people who tried to make a few pence out of it. There were old women who were accustomed to taking a saucepan of hot porter with a spoon or two of sugar going to bed every night. But digging, as the man said, will bring you to your senses and so it did in the case of the priest, and its effect persisted until his death. When after a good week's fishing the country people went to Dingle on a fair-day you would need the queen's army on the streets to keep those who had taken the pledge away from drinking porter and spreeing. The curate found that the seed he was trying to sow wasn't very fertile and when harvest-time came the spring work bore little fruit. He also found out that the parish priest was not as insistent on his parishioners taking the pledge, and so he was coming a bit more to his senses with each passing day.

If a man broke his pledge the curate would be on his doorstep as soon as he got wind of the word, and let neither God nor Mary grudge that poor devil the abuse the priest would give him. Quite often the priest was told a fair few lies and had it rammed down his throat that what he had been told was a downright lie.

There was a man north in Ballyferriter and any morning the priest made him take the pledge he had it broken in bits by nightfall. The priest went after him in determined mood, cornered him and ordered him go down on his knees and take the pledge again.

'There's no need, Father,' he said. 'May I be as dead as my mother who was buried above in the graveyard two days ago if I've broken the pledge.'

The priest let him go and went home. The following morning he was talking to a man from the same townland as the man who had spoken about his mother.

'I thought,' said the priest, 'that Dan above had broken the pledge, but his reply to me was that may he be as dead as his mother who was buried up there two days ago if he had broken the pledge.'

'If his mother was buried,' said the man to whom the priest was speaking, 'she wouldn't have been talking to me this morning.'

'Oh my!' said the priest, 'wait until I get a hold of him. It wasn't enough for him to break the pledge without making it worse by telling me lies.'

They say that for two months the pledge-man was afraid to go the parish Mass when the curate was celebrating, but if the curate was in Dunquin or in Carrig the man would go to Mass without any fear whatsoever. But the priest nabbed him on the strand one day when he was gathering seaweed, and they went very close to drowning one another because your man dragged the priest out into the water hoping he would let go his grip, but upon my word he didn't, and the priest made him take the pledge once more. Your man broke the pledge in bits again at the first opportunity, and said that he was receiving great support from the devil because the only thing on his mind was that the next time the priest put such pressure on him one or other of them would suffer serious consequences. The story goes that he was a big strapping man, as good a man as ever broke bread only that he had a love of drink and never got drunk on his own money but rather on that of foolish people.

The day dawned when the pledge-priest was transferred from Ballyferriter never to return because he had done more harm than good to the area. When the Ballyferriter man heard the welcome news he went down on his knees and spent quite a while praying to God that he would never again lay eyes on the priest and pouring curses down on top of the poor priest's head who was only doing what was best for him.

In those days many a poor woman used to bring a half-gallon and sometimes a gallon of whiskey down to the pier when their men were out fishing late and early. The pledge had put an end to that practice and those selling the drink had been deprived of the bit of money which helped them to make ends meet. They too went on their knees thanking God that their livelihood had been restored and they were free to resume the practice. They used to be away from home day and night selling the whiskey from pier to pier. No matter what the weather was like or whether the fishing was good or bad every man had his glass of whiskey after the night and needed it too. This young priest had no idea of the hardship endured by fishermen, but the old parish priest had, and that was the end of it. The pledge was a thing of the past throughout the area.

The police found out that drink was being sold in a speakeasy on the Island and so they made a raid and put a stop to it. Not surprisingly the pledge-priest didn't escape suspicion of having given the game away and the islanders were very annoyed with him as water was now the only thing they had to drink. The old women too were annoyed by the ban on porter because many is the good saucepanful of it they had poured down their gullets as had young children whom it saved from dying. A plan was needed and the plan was that you would buy a barrel of porter, bring it home and be drinking it at your ease until it was bottom up. Full barrels and half-barrels were available and most houses kept a half-barrel because it fitted neatly into a sack and nobody would take any notice of what the sack contained. If any house on the Island didn't have a half-barrel they could get all the porter they wanted from the people who had help to bring it in from the mainland. Whiskey was plentiful as it was the best of all to heat the fishermen after a night's fishing. As a man once said: 'I have whiskey and Nell has hot porter going to bed while the children are sound asleep from the beginning of the night thanks to hot porter sweetened with sugar.'

The police turned a blind eye to those half-kegs provided they weren't brought in too openly. Weren't they often brought in openly before that to weddings and wakes and the police ignored them?

Whenever an islander died the people would be very lonely for a month or so and once night fell you would see nobody outdoors. The old superstitions were still very much alive and no one spoke of anything else. If the pope himself were to come amongst them it is most unlikely that he could alter their ways and even if he did so they would have completely forgotten about it the following day.

The women from the mainland who had married into the Island had picked up a great amount of knowledge and experience from their servant days in various parts of the country and by taking note of how people on the mainland organised things. A death on the Island in olden times required the devil's own organising. If there was any kind of clock in the wake-house it was stopped the very moment the soul departed the body, and there would be no time in the house during the night unless somebody was wearing a watch, and that indeed was a rarity on the Island. I imagine that some people had never laid eyes on a watch. The person would be three hours dead before man or woman laid hands on him. When those three hours were up the corpse was groomed for eternity.

There were two or three women who were skilled in this work, women who were getting on in years, their families reared and they themselves too old to have any more children. I suppose they were well aware of these matters because of the superstitions concerning such women. Preparing the corpse and laying it out on two tables in the kitchen made for a hard day's work. Whether the kitchen was big or small they always had to have two tables. A blanket and a white sheet were placed under the corpse, a sheet or two were placed above it with another one reaching to the ground on the inside. Then three or four women would go to where the corpse was lying ready and washed, bring it over and lay it on the tables. To see the corpse stretched out and cleaner than it had been for twenty years you would have difficulty in recognising it.

There was a middle-aged man on the Island who used to clean-shave every old man who died. When he'd hear that the dead man was ready for shaving his heart would leap for joy and delight. And why not? Wouldn't he have plenty to eat and drink for a day and a night? He had a wonderful razor and was a great hand at sharpening and taking care of it and shaving the dead man just as neatly as if he was going to be married. He thought little of any razor that wasn't manufactured in Germany or in Hamburg. Those were made of the finest steel. Pilib didn't use a brush to lather the corpse, nothing but washing-soap, hard water that was quite hot and a reasonable amount of time to rub the soap in.

As soon as he put his foot on the floor of the wake-house a noggin of whiskey was waiting to be handed to him and I can assure you that far from refusing it he quickly poured it down his gullet. Then he was given a pipe and a cloud of smoke and vapour would fill the house reminding one of the Dingle train leaving the town with a load of stock on the evening of a fair-day. Having finished everything off his mind was at ease. He would take his razor in his hand and soon the corpse was shaved and cleaned. When that was done he would say: 'You're clean now, Pad, but who will shave the beard off Pilib, God help him?'

He would then go on his two knees and recite the prayers for the dead over the corpse. Another noggin of whiskey and a fog of smoke in the air, and if ever a man in Ireland was happy it was Pilib after his efforts. He was a big strong rugged man, kindly and charitable and never had an enemy on the Island. Tobacco and clay pipes were available and Pilib always cut the tobacco while two others rubbed it small enough for the pipes and another packed it into them. A certain number of pipes was sent with the corpse to the mainland and they had to be full to the brim for fear that a person might get one that wasn't properly filled and would curse the dead person.

After some pipes had been filled and given out around the house and everyone was fairly tired of sucking the tobacco the bucket of porter came around. It took a good man to carry the tobacco and porter together. After the porter was handed out there were lashings of white bread, fine strong tea and jam with two or three women waiting on the table.

Twelve o'clock midnight was the time to recite the Rosary of the Dead and there was always some old woman at the wake who would start off with a string of prayers before she began any decade. They would have consumed a good amount of drink by that time of night and some of them would be as happy to see the devil as to hear Nell beginning the Rosary. Nell would speak. 'Everybody on their knees. The Family Rosary is about to commence.' Naturally she would begin with 'In the name of the Father' and then the prayers for the dead person present and for those who had long ago gone the way of truth. However a sermon that is too long loses its effect and so too did Nell's big long prayers.

Pilib was one night in a wake-house. His belly was stuffed with food and drink in honour of the person who had died, and the strength of the drink was livening him up. He put his hand in his pocket, took out his beads and launched into the Rosary, but before he began the decade he spoke: 'Listen to herself and her squawking, with her belly so full of food and drink that you could kill a flea in her navel.'

Nell stopped. She hated nothing more than to hear Pilib talking in the wake-house. Pilib knew that Nell's Rosary would take too long and the men would be waiting too long for the porter-bucket. He was a real trickster and was well aware that everybody would be on his side.

6

The islandwomen worked very hard on the hill, on the strand and at tillage. With the coming of the spring tides they would be up to their navels in water hauling in strap wrack and bringing it up above the high-water mark. A husband would scarcely have cut a load when his wife would be back to collect it, throw it up on her back and carry it off up the beach, through rocks, through water and through large boulders. She didn't care as long as she had the seaweed. All the women worked equally hard while the spring tide lasted, returning home when it began to flow and bringing the seaweed to the fields with their donkeys while their menfolk threw it up to them on the top of the cliff. This continued for the three days the tides lasted.

It was the same with the turf. The men cut it but that was all they had to do with it. The women were the ones who saved it. Some of them were great hands at digging the soil with a spade and also at digging furrows and any man who a good wife had a good workhorse. The man lucky enough to have such a wife was much envied. One fellow would remark to another: 'What a woman he got!'

'He did indeed. Didn't his father know where he was going the day he made the match for him? The offspring of good women, boy!' Her work involved wool and flax and spindle thread, a weight and spinning wheel and knitting and sewing, washing wool and steeping and bleaching and pulling flax. Every day she rose from her bed her work was laid out before her, as the man said.

They had the very best of wool. They washed and cleaned it and brought it to the mill to have it rolled and carded. They used to have large sheets of it because they had to make thirty yards of flannel each year. Spinning went on from morning till night and even well into the night. The work wasn't as hard if there were two women in the house as one of them would take a turn at the spinning wheel and then another turn on the needles knitting socks and pullovers. If there were three women in the house the three of them would spin for pay and make money from their craft. They did the spinning during the winter season. A couple of houses had a warp frame and gave it out on loan because a day spent on the frame involved a lot of hard work. The frame would be set up against one wall of the house, with two women standing on either side of it and moving up and down. One woman would go half-way and the other would come to meet her, take the thread from her and put it on the felloe of the wheel. Two other women on the floor looked after the balls of wool and waited to see when the skein was used up to turn the balls in the right direction. A good part of the day would have passed by the time they finished with the wool. Then it was taken off the frame with the greatest care because if anything went wrong with the two ends all the work went for nothing and the wool was destroyed. The work needed to be in the hands of a knowledgeable woman who knew all about weaving. Then the wool was packed into a nice clean bag and brought to the weaver whose two eyes were wide open waiting for it. Believe you me the islandwomen didn't spend their time rubbing powder into themselves.

They pulled the flax from the ground when it shed its flowers, and it was left there for a week. There was a spot on the Island known as the Flax Wells where water sprang up out of the earth. They dammed the water by placing sods around its source and doing so meant that the place filled up with water. They would bring along the flax and put it into the water with stones on top of it and there it was left until it was as white as a swan. By this time too it was as soft as wool, and so they combed it well, teased it out and made it into balls with their cards which were steel-toothed. Two combs were needed to card the flax. A half-quern, as they say, can't grind on its own.

There was a special wheel for carding the flax. It wasn't at all as big as the wool-wheel. Some of the women were excellent spinners. The weaver would weave whatever you wished to have made, bed-sheets and table-cloths and pieces to be used as aprons and summer trousers for male children. The weaver also made sails that were ideal for the big boats because there was no chance that the wind could tear them, and of course that was the kind of sail which the boatmen needed. The women who made the sails to order were well paid for their work. Orders came from everywhere, so much so that they couldn't fulfil them all due to a shortage of material. Handling flax made for a great deal of hard work. It was impossible to do it without help, and like many other practices it too waned.

The women engaged in weaving were for the most part married women and each year they gave birth to a child. Such children were known as the spinning-wheel children because the women would have spent the whole night weaving before going to bed. Didn't the men show great sense?

It is said that at that time there was a thin dark-haired woman on the Island, for all the world like a tall thin bare stem of burnt heather and as hard as a piece of iron. People used to remark to one another: 'How does her husband allow her into his bed at all?' That was just talk, however. That dark-haired woman gave birth to four sets of twins one after the other, a set each year. Each set consisted of a male child and a female child, and they became known as the 'spinning-wheel family'. Those who were making fun of the father had to shut up. They had nothing to say. The facts were proved, the truth was there in front of their very eyes, and the twins were prancing around the fields.

The old people said that there was a twins-strain in her and that her father-in-law was second to none at matchmaking. It was rumoured that he spent a week on the mainland making a match for his son in an effort to find a wife with a twins-strain in her. When he saw the colour of the black woman's skin he thought that she wouldn't fill the bill, that his son wouldn't marry her. What did he do? He brought the son out and showed him a good-looking woman because he wouldn't lay eyes on her again until they would meet at the altar. Whatever the woman's colour when they met at the altar there was nothing he could do but accept her.

In each house on the Island there were always from seven to twelve in family. Only an odd house would have one or two, and very rarely indeed was there a couple without any. There wasn't another such place in Ireland. There were so many children coming from the Island for baptism that the parish priest said that only for the islandwomen he would have no child's name in the baptismal register. Quite frequently a child would be almost a year old before its parents would feel like baptising it, and they would wait for two or three children to be baptised together because then one horse and one messenger could handle the lot.

Child-birth was often difficult, but if so there was a certain man who was very experienced in bringing young calves and young lambs and young goats into the world. He was an expert at that work, and was known as the Rabbit Catcher. He always came when sent for, and like the bone-setter of today he was a master-hand at bringing children into the world.

The childbed was always in the corner of the kitchen. A boat-sail would be attached to the rafters and arranged so as to make a small room as you might say. The floor inside was then covered with bedding and straw or dry ferns and the woman who was due to give birth was left to roll about as she wished. Many is the good man and woman who came into the world on the Island in that type of childbed. Once the woman had given birth to the child she wasn't to be seen again until nine days later by which time she was ready to race again.

A woman was in her childbed on the Island one time.

'I hear,' said Diarmaid to Tom,' that Big Nora was in her childbed to have another child but that she was having difficulty.'

'Wait a while,' said Tom, 'until the Rabbit Catcher hears about it. He'll bring along his fine hot seal-oil and by the time he's finished with her Nora will loft the child over to Beginis with one single volley.'

Years ago when times were not so good a bad winter storm drove a sailing vessel ashore on the northern side of the Island, and when some man or other looked towards the Pass of the Slope he noticed that the sea was full of big white lumps. He wondered what they were and thought that they were sheep which the previous night's wind had blown over the cliff. He returned home and told his story. A boat was launched and off with them back to the Sorrowful Slope where the man had seen the lumps, but on coming close the crew saw clearly that they weren't sheep. They grappled with them and hauled one or two chunks on board. On seeing the stuff they were straightaway convinced that it was butter. A second boat arrived and then a third and they were loaded to the gunwale with the fine fragrant butter. They brought it back to the pier and it was then they found out what they really had. A woman who had spent a long time in America working in a woollen mill explained to them that it was in fact yellow oil.

They scarcely waited to listen to her. Every woman and man on the Island hurried to collect the oil and store it. 'Wasn't it God who sent it their way,' said an old woman, 'food for man and child?' There was never anything like it for cooking rabbits. The toughest and oldest buck-rabbit when cooked in the yellow oil tasted as nice as a young one. They used the oil on the yellow bread in the morning and it was great for softening that same bread, particularly for those whose teeth weren't at all sound. They used it with potatoes in the middle of the day and at night, and when ever they put a bite into their mouths they had to have the yellow grease with it. Women and children continued to use it while it lasted, and you can take it from me that nobody complained of constipation or urine problems. Everything was moving like a stream of water down the side of a hill.

Houses didn't have the conveniences then that they have now and when you got a call of nature, no matter what time of night it was, you had to go outdoors, turn your arse to the fence and spray the grass. Everyone in the house had to do likewise. Even the woman of the house herself had to run when, as the man said, the pressure came.

A woman got a call of nature one night and she knew nothing until the pressure came on her from both sides. She went out, headed for the yard and dumped the load. She never expected anything until she spotted the little baby under her legs. She screamed and roared and Tom wasn't long coming to her aid. He had everything ready in no time, the woman and the child deposited in the corner and the midwife brought to the house, but her presence wasn't required because the yellow oil had loosened the bonds on the baby. He was the man for the job, I tell you.

The midwife put a lighting piece of cloth on the baby's navel after she had cleaned and washed him. She then placed him on his mother's breast and he immediately started feeding. 'Upon my soul, Mary,' said he, 'the child brought the colour straight from the mother!' The child was as yellow as could be, and that wasn't hard for him because neither the mother or father was too good-looking, apart altogether from the yellow putty.

A second child came and then a third. As well as that the midwife was busy washing and cleaning and dressing them but that was all she had to do because whenever the pressure came on the mother the child was on the straw much faster than an egg from a hen. And why not? Hadn't the lubrication inside made it easy for everything to come out? While the yellow oil lasted every child born on the Island took its colour from it.

The mothers always brought their children to Ballyferriter to be baptised because no child in those days had a teat or a bottle. If a child screamed or yelled the mother simply opened the button, pulled out her nipple, stuck it into the child's mouth and left him to feed away until such time as he fell sound asleep.

Three children were one time brought north to Ballyferriter church. The priest came out. He wasn't too nice or too civil because the mothers were poor and had little gold or riches hanging to them. The children were placed together so that the same words would do the three but when the priest saw the colour of them he nearly fainted because he had never previously seen the like of them. He asked each mother umpteen questions, where did she get the child, who was the father and where did the colour come from. He thought that maybe sailors from China had been shipwrecked and had come to the Island and that they had a hand in the colour. 'I wouldn't be long talking to him,' said Peg, 'when I'd throw the child to him be-damned and let him look after him.'

When the other children went north to be baptised he was not the same priest at all. He had learned a thing or two from the sacristan. As people say, there was never a good priest who did not have an able sacristan.

Life was going very well on the Island in those days. We are told that no man, woman or child died there for forty-five years thanks to the yellow oil which got rid of every germ and worm in the people. It isn't hard to believe that.

Those first three yellow-coloured children whom the priest in Ballyferriter baptised were well past pension-age when the pension first came out. The three of them went north to get proof of their age, but even if the priest and the sacristan were still poring over the register they couldn't find anyone by the name of

Pad. They had to return home and if the deceased priest and the living priest and the sacristan weren't cursed roundly then nobody ever was. What really riled them was the fact that people born three and six months after them were knocking a great rattle out of their pensions. They had driven the priest to distraction and he asked a few shrewd people if they had any idea as to whether those good men were of pension age. The only evidence they could provide was that the children born after them were drawing the pension and that that year was the year of the yellow putty. The priest returned home, took all the necessary steps and they soon received their pensions. Even if it was small at least they had it.

The period of the yellow oil on the Island lasted only a while just like everything else. It wasn't being grown or planted there and constant use brings an end to even that which is in large supply. So it was in the case of the yellow oil that came in as wrack. When it was all used up and no longer greasing the stomachs of either young or old their bowels weren't working all that well generally speaking. Those advanced in age were coming off worst and were falling away because there was nothing good coming out of their stomachs. That period was known to the old people as the 'time of the pebbles' because they were often unable for two, three or perhaps even four days to pass anything other than a few tiny pebbles. As one man said: 'After waiting a week all I could pass were sheep's droppings.'

A herb called senna was growing on the Island at that time and was highly regarded as a laxative. Every house there used to steep and boil it and men, women and children drank a mugful of it every morning. The old men and women drank seawater too but instead of loosening the women it made them completely constipated. They had to give up using it and go back to the senna again. Salts were unknown in those days and were it not for some woman in Dingle every old man and woman on the Island would have died from constipation. Salts came in pound packets and were used more widely even than milk. Salts brought them relief, something they badly needed.

7

The first inhabitants of the Western Island had horses and ploughing equipment, and the traces of their ploughing and labours are still to be seen on the south side of the Island and will, I imagine, be there for as long as the Island remains above water. The land on the south side is as fertile as any in Ireland, its only drawback being that it is very exposed. Those people mostly sowed potatoes, oats and barley. They threshed the oats with flails and ground it with querns.

Their greatest fear was that the potatoes might fail. They usually had enough potatoes to last from one end of the year to the other and while they had them they were on the pig's back, but the day came when the potato crop failed. Then there was hullabaloo. They were badly off for potatoes and meal but not half as badly off as the unfortunate people on the mainland.

Whatever number died on the Island during the Famine none of them died of hunger but rather from some other disease, but whether they died of disease or something else hunger was blamed for it. During the really bad times great luck came the islanders' way. A large ship laden with wheat was wrecked off the coast of the Island and most of its cargo was thrown up on the White Strand. Every man, woman and child was engaged in bringing the wheat home in bags and panniers carried by the donkeys. They dried it, an easy task as it hadn't yet absorbed the sea-water. That ship and its cargo rescued the islanders from hunger. The story of that vessel has been on people's lips ever since the day she struck the reef, and many is the prayer that was said in gratitude to God and on behalf of the sailors who were drowned.

The potato-seed on the Island wasn't too good after the Famine and the great blight. 'Blacks' were the commonest variety sown. They were good potatoes, nice to eat and stood up well to the wind but this particular year they failed because they were being set over too long a period in practically the same ground. Word went out that they had failed. There was a gentleman in Limerick who sent out an appeal asking all the farmers of the county to donate half-sacks of potatoes which he himself would then send by boat to the Island. The boat arrived from Limerick laden to the rail with lovely potatoes called Champions. Those with large families were given two or perhaps three bagfuls after everybody else had got a fair share. There weren't even twenty households on the Island then nor for a long time afterwards.

The Champions boat kept them going for a long time. Thanks were expressed to the man who had come to their aid, and he was sent on his way with blessings, not to mind the prayers of the old women. The Champions were boiled with dried mackerel. When the potatoes and the fish, and milk if the family happened to have some, were put on the table everybody was so busy devouring them that not a word was spoken. Nothing was left on the table. Even the fish-scales were eaten and the table itself barely escaped the same fate. No finer potatoes ever came to the Island but badly and all as seed potatoes were needed there weren't many left when the time came to set them.

'Mother Mary,' said one man, 'you couldn't stop. Weren't we eating them from day till morning, and we'd have eaten more only that we had to spare them for seed. And look what happened! We forgot completely about the seed. Now I haven't as much as one to set. I'll have to strike off south with my bag tomorrow.' He returned having got plenty of them. His old folk were always kind and they wouldn't give it to anyone to say that they left him without.

Cows and milk were plentiful on the Island. They also had goats long ago, and they themselves mostly used goat's milk because they used to put the cow's milk in coolers so as to have home-made butter. They gave the goat's milk to the young children except in the case of a strong healthy woman whose own milk was good and nourishing. Very often such a woman's child didn't drink any goat's milk until the age of two or more.

Any child who remained a long time at the breast was known as a yellow *slibire* or lanky child but I guarantee you that when that child got a bit older there wasn't a child in the village as healthy or as fair-skinned. Even his teeth remained healthy and he retained all of them until he died. He never suffered from whooping cough or measles. Neither frost nor snow affected him. In fact he was always out in all sorts of weather. Children reared on cow's milk suffered from some disease or affliction daily.

The islanders knew nothing about diseases or how to cure them. 'Live if that's what is destined for you, and if it isn't pass on.' That was what they used to say and indeed there was nothing else they could say.

Life improved in due course. As an islandman once said, white bread, pig's feet and the Bandon Rattler are the best food of all. You'd see children up and down the paths in those days with half a pig's foot or the nose of a Danish pig's head in their hands and grease back to their ears. When an old man would see them he would say: 'Indeed, child, your great-grandfather didn't have much grease from pig's feet or pig's head on him because he never got a taste of them.'

When the women went to the hill to foot or rick turf they brought pig's feet and white bread with them and only for the dogs that used to roam the hill I imagine that the bones of those same pig's feet would be there until this very day. The women would bring five or six big bottles of water with them because those pig's feet, since they are salted, create an awful thirst.

Three kinds of flour were to be had and yellow meal that contained a lot of oil. Those women would add a couple of saucers of flour to a fair amount of the yellow meal and mix them together with some soda. They made their own yeast and you could not get the likes of it anywhere in Ireland. When making the yeast they used to boil water. They would then pour the boiling water into an earthenware vessel that would take about a gallon, add a few saucers of flour and mix it until it all dissolved in the water. They then added a little grain of salt and a few large spoons of sugar. They put some potatoes on the fire to boil and mashed those boiled potatoes on a plate until they were as fine as the flour. The whole lot was mixed together until it was liquid. The vessel was placed beside the fire and left there for three or four days after which time it was sufficiently sour to wet the cake with it. That yeast was second to none.

The islandwomen were excellent bakers as were also some of the men. Visitors to the Island when having a bite to eat could not resist the bread, it was so lovely and tasty. Many is the curse that was poured on top of the heads of some of them because they would devour all the bread that had been baked, and all the thanks one got from them was: 'May God leave ye the health!' Then the woman of the house would have to put down another big fire, get a dish, flour and the white flour – that is what they called the yeast – and make and bake another cake. There was often a good battle between a man and his wife regarding that same meal, because very often it was the man who had invited the fellow who cleared everything on the table, and Cáit or whatever the woman's name was would then have good reason to talk.

The high standard of the bread on the Island was well known and the people on the mainland wondered how it could be as tasty as it was reputed to be. The islanders' relatives on the mainland often came in and they were never very anxious to leave. 'Yerrah, stay another week,' the islandwoman would say to them. No sooner said than done. They would gorge themselves with food as they had nothing else to do except chatter and talk nonstop. That was not surprising. In the end the islandwomen's only fear was that the relatives would have to be tied just like the cows to send them home. Hadn't they tasted the pasture, and only a stepmother would blame them for leaving it! On seeing them departing from the Island you would swear that a mother or father of nine had died, such was their wailing and crying. The men who brought them to Dunquin often cursed them profusely because some of them were bursting with food.

'How well not one of those bitches comes in,' said one man, 'until we've bound every sheaf of the harvest!'

'You're right,' replied another man. 'Wasn't it the likes of those who were too wily for Aristotle, so why wouldn't they be too wily for us?'

Those women, however, deserved a good turn because many is the bite the islanders got from them when they were stranded on the mainland by the weather.

Liam Ó Lúing, a shop-keeper from Ballyferriter and a great man for Irish, brought much happiness to the Island. He used to send flour, meal, tea, sugar, salt, meat and pig's feet even, to a certain house in Dunquin for the islanders who badly needed them. They found it difficult at first to accept this good man because they were already in the grip of merchants in Dingle, and there was nothing to be got from the man in Ballyferriter without cash down, and he was dead right.

He was all the time sending them all sorts of goods over the Gap of Carhoo including the nicest pig's heads that ever came to the Island and flitches of bacon about an inch and a half high and four feet long. That meat was known as Danish. The period was known as the 'roast period', an accurate description. There wasn't a house on the Island that hadn't two flitches of bacon and a couple of Danish heads hanging down on either side of the hob. There were two roasting ovens and a fairly large skillet for boiling rabbits because rabbits were better and tastier if they were first boiled and then roasted. The pig's heads were quite cheap, about a half-crown each, but a man with a right good appetite would have no trouble in devouring one of them at one meal, with perhaps half a rabbit as well. Food is the work-horse as they say.

Liam Ó Lúing's business was increasing from day to day and when a certain man from Dunquin saw the extent of Liam's business he approached another shopkeeper and they agreed that the Dunquin fellow would cart goods to his own house and sell them to the islanders. No sooner said than done. This fellow had relatives on the Island and of course birds of a feather flock together. A second man from Dunquin made an agreement with another merchant in Dingle, and so the race began. Within two years there were four shops in Dunquin selling all sorts of goods which were being sent to them by those big Dingle merchants.

The man from Ballyferriter then began paying frequent visits to the Island as he felt that his business was going down. His turnover wasn't as large as it had been in previous years because the other shop-keepers were undermining it. He landed on the pier one day, pulled out quite a large-sized piece of cardboard, and pulled over his head and down on to his shoulders the strap attached to the cardboard which revealed the words 'Credit Forever' neatly written in Irish. He had never before given anything on credit. It was always cash down, but competition was hotting up and he had to make some move, though it didn't come from his heart because he had read the history of the Island a long time previously. When the pressure is on the old hag she has to run for it and so it was with the man from

Ballyferriter.

That was the time when the islanders were on the pig's back. Liam loosened the purse-strings. Events underwent a great change. The shopkeepers in Dunquin were left with no choice but to follow his lead or lose the battle. That was easy for them because they were using their own spurs on other people's horses. They were selling the goods, not buying them, but Liam Ó Lúing was buying as well as selling. He was the one who started the race whichever horse was going to win it.

It was easy to set up a little house in those days as it was just a matter of 'Hold out your bag, Micheál.' A half-sack of flour and a half-sack of very wholesome meal cost twenty shillings. The islanders would pay a pound now and again and put three pounds in a purse for their own rainy day. The result was they hadn't enough bags to put all the goods into. Those were great times, as Pad said.

The man in Ballyferriter was giving out and complaining and went to the Island on many a Sunday in an effort to collect some of the old debts. He wasn't hard on the poor but he didn't spare those who he knew had money.

That was the time when the Island was on the map of happiness. As the man from Kildurrihy said after spending a few days on the Island, in every house he visited they were eating food fit for a priest. It was quite easy too for an islandman to get a wife because women were plentiful on the mainland but they had nowhere to go and so their parents were throwing them int the faces of the islandmen. Many of them came in and each one was as healthy and as strong as a she-donkey. It was just as well because they had to carry everything on their backs, particularly seaweed and bags of mussels. They weren't afraid to tackle any job. How could they be so since they were being plied with food and showing all the signs of it? Hadn't they got what they wanted, a good husband and nourishing food?

The old generation were surprised at how good life was to their grandchildren compared to themselves. Those grandchildren often told them that their skin still bore the signs of the yellow meal and potatoes and fish but what the old people said in response made a lot of sense. 'I'm telling ye that ours is the most lasting and healthiest of all skins.'

Later events proved that they were right. The younger generation's teeth soon began to rot. They would have an ear-ache today and two other aches tomorrow, and if they were caught out in a shower on the hill or at sea it meant two days in bed. It was nothing but colds, sore throats and coughs, whereas those with the yellow skin knew nothing about those illnesses in their youth. It is said that those illnesses began with the fourth generation of islanders.

8

According as the children on the Island were growing up to be men and women the population became so great that they had to go their various ways seeking a livelihood in the great world outside. Some went east, some west, some north and some south. Many of the girls married whatever kind of man came along, some of them good men but most of them miserable creatures. So it was too with the men who left the Island. They were good fishermen and settled down near the coast and made a good living out of fishing. Life wasn't as hard during their time as it had been during the time of previous generations. Granted the pay was small but things were almost for nothing and everything was as plentiful as water. Anybody with any bit of life in him could survive.

Others went across the sea to America. They had no option. There was no money to be got on the side of the road in America then or for quite sometime afterwards, but the islanders were accustomed to hardship and put up with it. They accepted whatever type of work they could get. Mills and the railway were their preferences with the women working in the mills and the men on the railway. As soon as ever they had saved the cost of the fare they sent it to a sister or a brother who was still at home to enable them to follow. America was for them the college and the university in those days. The strength and spirit of the Island began to wane as people were growing old and many of them were going to their eternal reward. Couples who had reared nine children on the Island were soon left with just one and even that child was only waiting for those who had emigrated to come to his aid and rescue him from the sinking ship. Some of them were successful over there while others did not do quite so well. They lacked learning and education and their knowledge of English was almost non-existent. They were no better than animals. Whenever a ganger or overseer ordered them to do something or other he might as well have been speaking to a donkey or a horse. One thing stood to them, however, they were good workers. Of course the islanders weren't the only group in America who had no English. The Italians and the French were in the same situation and that encouraged the islanders.

Some people who left the Island never returned. Their parents and relatives had passed on. All their property was in the hands of others and their houses had fallen down since there was nobody to put a roof or scollop on them. Those in America who were experiencing poor health and became ill were ordered by their doctor to return home to the old sod since the air over there didn't suit them. They came home, both men and women. They came to live again on the Island and very shortly after their return their health was restored. They settled down, married and were doing very well. Once their health improved there was no stopping them.

They had seen enough of America, and the hard times there made them wish to live again on this Island. They reared large families, their children attended the school which was then the best in Ireland, and there was nobody under the age of forty on the Island who wasn't the equal of anyone in the country at writing, reading and arithmetic in both Irish and English. A person going to America at that time had to undergo a medical examination and very importantly a test in reading and writing. Nevertheless nobody went from the Island to Cobh in County Cork who didn't pass with flying colours, whereas many from the mainland were sent home, mostly because they had neither reading nor writing. When the islanders landed in America they had little difficulty in finding work.

There was one particular young lad from the Island who went to America. He wasn't fully eighteen years old when leaving. He had an uncle in Springfield who took him under his wing and set him on the right road. For a full year he sent him to night-school after he had finished his day's work, and the young lad being such a good student had no difficulty with his studies. When he first arrived there he was employed in a bicycle-shop and after three years the bosses put him in charge of the shop and of all the staff as well. He spent all his life working in that shop and gave employment to every young chap who went from the Island to Springfield. He was very successful. He paid a visit or two home and when he was leaving his eyes were anything but dry and he often remarked that all the gold in the world couldn't buy the happiness to be got from one's native place. He was absolutely right because many others returned to their native sod and remained there.

Any family with a member in America was on the pig's back because the old couple never stopped complaining to them, and most of their complaints were a pack of lies. People who were getting letters were much envied, not surprisingly because those letters were chock-full of dollars or so it was said. As soon as boys and girls became old enough to travel they only had to send for their fare to their relatives over there.

There were two middle-aged women on the Island at that time who worked hard at the well, on the hill and on the strand, and also helping their brothers and their brothers' wives to rear their families. They were being worked to the bone. The two met one day at the well. A third woman came along. The two mischiefmakers could talk of nothing else but the letters which were coming from America. Both were named Mary and one Mary said to the other: 'Mary, it will be a long time before any letter comes to either of the two of us.'

The other Mary answered her in a calm gentle voice with a real witty remark. 'Take that now, Mary, because we didn't sow seed in our soil as did those who are getting the letters!'

'It is too late now for you to be talking of your soil or your seed since you didn't sow them when you were in the spring-time of life,' the other Mary replied.

The third woman never uttered a word because she was getting letters and knew well that the two Marys were dangerous hairpins. The less said the better, as the man from Dunquin said long ago. The letters continued to come for a long time afterwards until finally the people in America realised that those at home were putting together a lot more money than they themselves were.

The Island was thriving at the beginning of this century. In the words of the man from the mainland they had gold and silver and no scarcity of women. There was no one then going anywhere to try and make a shilling. They could make it on their own doorstep, but there was also the odd one among them who rushed off to America and if they did some of them didn't even last three months there. On returning home many of them were mad for work and fishing. They had learned a thing or two over there and as some of them said to those who had never left the Island: 'You must go to America if you wish to survive.' They snapped up every available woman from Annascaul west, married her and brought her into the Island and five or six sheep along with her.

One of those fellows was a small man who returned home after six months in America. He wasn't fully five feet in height. He left the Island one day during Shrovetide and nobody was any the wiser until he arrived home married to a big strapping wife who was as broad as she was tall. An old islander was looking at her and when she had gone a short distance past him he turned around and said: 'Your soul to the devil, didn't he get a right one? He won't have to worry about what kind of a load he puts on her because she's well able to carry it. Hasn't she the rear end of a horse? Lads,' he said to the men listening to him who hadn't married, 'ye'll have to go to America if ye wish to get anywhere. Hasn't that terrier of a man great courage to take on such a chunk of a woman?'

A man who had spent five years in a rubber-shop in America returned home. He was the nicest man that ever left the Island for America but when he returned his own family didn't recognise him nor indeed did anybody else. Nobody would believe that he was the same Tadhg. He was thin and spare, nothing but skin and bone. There was no word to describe his colour. An old islandwoman nick-named him 'The Black Man' and the name stuck until the day he died, but his death and baptism were many years apart because he lived so long that he had nearly driven the people on the Island out of their minds with the stories he brought home, most of which he himself had made up. When the weather was bad he would go from house to house telling those stories.

One day he was in a particular house. He was talking about hell. He told the people of the house that he had spent five years working in hell in America with a scorching fire on either side of him sending red sparks up in the air, and if one of them touched you it would burn you to ashes and you would never again be found. Some of them believed him while others left him and walked out the door. He said that hell was here in this world and not down below, that the first ever devil was born up in heaven and they were all sent down into this world and that anyone seeing them as he had would realise that America was full of them. But the change which had come over him within five years made the islanders wonder what had caused him to be black and where did his flesh and his healthy appearance go. He was forever holding forth in that way until one day he met an old woman on the Island. When he had finished speaking she said: 'Tadhg, God brought you to America and the devil brought you back home but if you continue as you are you won't have God or the devil here or there because there's nothing coming out of your mouth but lies,' and she threw a half-pint of holy water on him.

That put an end to Tadhg's gallop that day but not to what Tadhg had his eye on. This old woman had a daughter who wasn't too good-looking. She had a nice little house and a tidy bit of land and that was Tadhg's main reason for going to the house with his yarns. He hadn't been calling there since he got the belt of the bottle but he took things nice and easy because he had learned that her fine girl of a daughter wasn't in any great demand. Tadhg had the name of money as has everybody who sets foot on the Golden Land. This old woman's daughter was very angry with her mother for having put the run on Tadhg and the word went round the village. Tadhg heard it too and it went down well with him.

'I'm always hearing,' he said, 'that the devil is alive and kicking in any house where there are only women because women aren't really right in the head until they have some sort of a man under the roof of the house.'

An account reached him from the woman who had broken the holy water bottle on his poll that she had a nice daughter and that they would be happy if he felt like lying with her. The baits were put out and the race was due to be run any day, and to be run quickly too while the iron was hot. Tadhg would re-mind you of nothing but a rabbit running away from a dog and thinking he would never make the burrow because he had nothing in the world in his pocket except just enough to pay the priest. The happy day came for Tadhg and the two women, and he was accepted into the fold without as much as a word being said against him.

9

A stranger once came to the Island and wanted to spend a few weeks there but no house wished to take him in nor indeed was he causing them any concern because they were tormented by people coming to spy on them for the landlord's stewards. Someone finally took pity on him and told him that he would share his own bed with him if he was agreeable. All this man wanted was to be indoors from the night-sky and get a bite to eat sometime during the day. He told the man of the house that he was a writer and that writing was his livelihood. He spent a fortnight on the Island and wrote about everything which he witnessed with his own two eyes. Having written about all that was to be seen he went off out by sea again.

That man's name was John Synge, the first stranger ever to holiday on the Island. He wrote down exactly and accurately everything as he had seen it. Every word that came from his pen was a true picture and those people from the Island who had come up a bit in the world after Synge's time and read his book had nose-bleeds because he didn't write about things that weren't there for him to see. Had he been inventing stories his work would not ring true and I think that his description of some of them flattered them.

After Synge left Cormac Ó Cadhlaigh arrived but he had a good smattering of Irish. Even so the islanders had their ears cocked listening to him. He spent his time in the company of the old people listening to them as they talked amongst themselves and writing down old stories and old sayings from them.

The island houses in those days weren't suitable for keeping visitors but those visitors didn't mind as long as they were taken in and given the same food as the islanders themselves ate. Visitors weren't charged thirty shillings a week. The charge was a mere ten shillings a week which was great money at that time. From then on the islanders weren't at all afraid of visitors. Bess and Clara, the landlord's agents, were under the sod and young islanders were dancing to music on their own land. That is how the wheels of this world rotate.

A young energetic man came one time and was accompanied by another man who was not too athletic. The young man was a dancing instructor and a teacher of Irish, and Roger, the old fellow accompanying him, was a fiddler. The young man sent out word that there would be Irish dancing in the school that night from eight o'clock until half-past ten and nobody would be charged as much as a half-penny. I imagine that if there was a charge there wouldn't be too much dancing. All the people came at the appointed time and your man began his one two three, one two three and tapped the floor behind him twice with his right leg. The old man played as directed by the instructor but the locals preferred the musician to the man teaching the dancing. One of the men looking on, when he saw the capers of the two of them, said: 'Well if there's bread and butter to be made out of any business this is surely it.' Not everyone, however, felt the same way. Some of them were interested and many picked up a good few steps and reels.

They spent a week in that manner and on the second last night the instructor announced that this was their livelihood, that neither of the two of them had any other income whatsoever. When the final night came your man got the deaf ear and only a few people who had a decent streak in them came to the school, and take my word for it that they didn't have much hanging to them any more than those who stayed at home. The two men left on the following day which was Sunday and neither God nor the devil ever saw either of them again. That is when a man in Ballyferriter remarked that if the two knew the islanders as well as himself did they would have stayed far away from them. Bought sense is best if you have somewhere to keep it but not many people have. Still and all it is well to have it.

There was a young lad on the Island at that time who had just begun his first season fishing. Not surprisingly, since he was fishing with his father, he didn't make much money. He became very interested in music, particularly in the fiddle, and to cap it all his father was the Island's best ever singer. This chap was one day sent to Dingle on some errand or other and whatever house he visited Roger was there playing for all he was worth. Your man fell madly in love with the fiddle and asked Roger if he would sell it to him. Roger replied that he wouldn't sell that particular fiddle but that he had two more at home and he would sell him one of them. His heart inside him leapt and he asked Roger to bring it along if it wasn't too dear.

'I've one for a pound,' said Roger, 'and another for two pounds and now since you are only a young lad I'll give you the two pound one for thirty shillings.'

'It's a bargain,' said the young fellow. 'Bring it along and when I'm going home I'll give the money to the man of the house.'

So it was. Roger brought along the fiddle and handed it in over the counter. The young lad called for the fiddle that evening. The woman of the house handed it over to him and asked him where was the money.

'Oh,' said the lad, 'I paid him early this morning, my good woman, when he came looking for it.'

'Everything is all right so,' she said.

'It is indeed,' said the lad, putting the fiddle under his arm and hitting the road west. Of course he hadn't paid as much as a brown half-penny for it. He brought it to the Island where the fiddle was most welcome though there was no one there who could knock any music out of it.

That night a woman was about to go to bed. Whatever glance she gave at the water-bucket she noticed that there was not a drop in the bottom of it. She wouldn't go to bed unless there was water in the house. It was almost the dead of night and she wasn't at all happy about having to go outdoors, but she would have to think of some plan and not go to bed without a drop of water in the shack. She and her husband used to sleep in a stretcher-bed in the corner. He was already in bed snoring like a pig. 'I pray God,' she said, 'that it may be your last sleep!' and she went out the door with her bucket and saucepan. She went off up to the well at the top of the village, filled the bucket with water and headed down home, but as she was passing Pats' house she heard the fiddle being played inside though there wasn't a sign of a light there. She stopped for a moment to know exactly where the music was coming from and found out handy enough that it was indeed coming from Pats' house. She knew well that some of the islanders had been in Dingle that day and she thought that perhaps Roger had come with them to stay for a while. She went in home to find her old fellow sitting on his backside in the bed and pulling so hard on the pipe that he was sending smoke as high as the mantelpiece.

'Look, Máire,' he said, 'it's true about the moon. It's full tonight and look how it has affected you.'

'My curse on the likes of you anyhow,' said Máire. 'How well it is the like of you should be talking! Sure there's no need at all for the moon to come out to set you going! Haven't you lost the run of yourself everyday of the week? Isn't that in your breeding and your nature?'

That was all there was to it because Máire was dying to tell her story about Roger. She began telling the old fellow what she had seen and heard but she might as well have been talking to the side of the bed as talking to Dan. Still and all her story impressed him. He went out early next morning and inquired of the first man he met: 'Is Roger after coming back again?'

'Yerrah, my good man,' said the other fellow, 'don't the dogs of the village know that neither God nor man will ever again see Roger here, because after spending a long fortnight playing music for them he didn't get a penny when he looked for payment.'

'My Máire,' said Dan, 'has lost her wits. It was she who told me that Roger was playing the fiddle in Pats' house about twelve o'clock last night.'

'That is a ridiculous story,' said the other man and left him there.

Dan was still like a hen with an egg and he wasn't too happy with the response. He strolled off west and spent a while going to and fro. When he got tired of being out and meeting nobody he headed for Pats' house and as he was passing the door what did he think he heard only Roger scratching the fiddle!

'Upon my soul, Máire,' he said, 'you're not as simple as I thought. If anyone is bothered I'm the one.'

He returned home meek and mild just like a child after spending the day mitching from school because he was afraid that Máire might give him a good lash of her tongue. All was quiet until a stupid old woman from the village dropped in. When Máire asked her if she had any news she replied: 'The devil a bit at all, except that Tadhg' – he was her husband – 'said that Roger arrived last night.'

Máire spoke because she was on the windward side of Dan, and Dan got a right scolding from her.

'I suppose,' said the stupid old woman, 'the poor devil came to collect his bit of money.'

'Indeed, God knows, praise and thanks be to Him, he'll have his gut out for a while waiting for it.'

Dan hated the thought of anyone coming to collect money from him. He was tight with money.

The fiddle was being tuned and scraped and it sounded like a cat or a corncrake or whatever other noise was being made with it. For all the people knew then Roger could be in the village. Pats had two young school-going daughters and they were the ones who let the fly out of the box. They said that they had a fiddle of their own, that Mike had brought it from Dingle and that he used to play it away non-stop every night after returning from fishing.

That was the first fiddle of their own which the islanders had. Mike didn't take long to learn it and knock traditional music out of it. He was a fine dancer also, and it was always said that a musician who can't dance can't be a good musician. Mike crossed the sea to America but didn't forget to bring the sliver with him. He got a job there like everyone else and used to take up the sliver every night. The islanders always called the fiddle a sliver because that is what it is shaped like. He wasn't very long over there when the word spread that a top-class musician had arrived from Kerry and could play every reel and jig that was ever played back home. He was invited to parties all over the city by Irish people who had long ago emigrated and were dying to hear Irish traditional music again.

That is how it was with Mike for a couple of years. A man approached him who used to rent a hall for Irish dancing. He appointed your man as full-time musician with no responsibilities whatsoever except to play there three nights a week. The hall was so popular that it became too small but the musician got a share in the new one and easy money began to flow his way. He spent many years playing there and made a fortune. But easy money brings its own problems and in the end even gold couldn't slake his thirst.

There were two other lads who learned to play the fiddle

with Mike on the Island but when he took his fiddle with him to America that was the end of their music. They were fishing, and if so as soon as they had made the price of a fiddle they bought one each. They were well able to play it though not as well as Mike because he could dance and arrange the music to suit the dancing. The other two couldn't dance but could play to their hearts' content.

All the lads on the Island were becoming interested in the fiddle and some of them set about making one. They succeeded too. Some of their fiddles were excellent while others were only fair. A father remarked to his son who had made one: 'I'd prefer to take up the sliver itself rather than that old thing you're after making.'

They made strings out of fishing-net cord to see what noise or music they could knock out of them and if the fiddle made any sound at all they put proper strings on it. Within a few years there was a sliver in every house in the village where there was a young girl or boy. In any house where there were five or six in the family each one played his own tune on the sliver. Consequently there wasn't a boy or girl on the Island who couldn't knock some smattering of music out of it.

One particular year a visitor came to the Island and remained a couple of weeks. All he wanted was music and women and dancing, and he got his fill of all three almost from daybreak and from nightfall until morning again. On returning home he sent a fiddle to everyone who had an old sliver. Many of them attempted to play the fiddle but only a few were successful. They had nobody but themselves to teach them and a person who can teach himself is a very rare individual. Only four lads on the whole Island succeeded in tuning and playing it properly. Only two of those are alive today and neither lives on the Island.

There was a melodeon too in every home in which there was a young girl or boy, and they were all able to play it and dance as well. Roger had left his mark on the dancing though he was poorly compensated. Still the seed which he sowed grew until it finally died through neglect. Another man with a melodeon came. He was well able to knock Irish music out of it. Every night a dance was held in the house where he was staying which meant that the young boys and girls used to be out almost until morning. They had little else to do during the day except to bring a couple of loads of turf from the hill and dress themselves up for the night. On fine nights the girls would bring the box-player back to the Spur at Seal Cove where there was a large area with room enough for two sets to be danced at the same time, and many other activities if you so wished! The young people then growing up on the Island were neither saints nor angels and they knew as much about the facts of life as others like them throughout the country. You can't beat nature, as the old woman said.

The girls and the boys preferred dancing outdoors to indoors but good things don't last too long and the mothers found out that the Spur was the place where the box-man was providing the fun.

There were two women on the Island and each had two daughters fit to be married. When the women heard about the capers they put their heads together to find out how they might bring this carry-on to an end. They collected two big bucketfuls of fine strong stale urine which gave off a steam that would knock a donkey. They put on their shawls and off they went with their two bucketfuls of urine. They never stopped nor rested until they reached the dancing-place. Your man was playing away while the others danced. One of the women threw her bucketful down on top of the box-player's head and the other threw hers on the dancers.

They all began screaming because the urine got into their eyes and no one could tell where anyone else was. The musician almost toppled over the cliff. When they recovered they went off home and that was the end of the Spur at Seal Cove.

But alas and the sins within my breast, neither that much stale urine nor twice as much of it again could keep the boys and girls away from one another or from dancing with one another either. The old ways were coming to an end and the new ways taking over and a mother might as well have been pouring water through a sieve as to be advising her family. Stranger followed stranger bringing with them dancing and music, but not even a dog could survive the summer heat in the little houses, so the music and the people took to the outdoors again. The two women, however, didn't go next or near them as they had been warned that if they did so they would be sent home stark naked. They became afraid and said to themselves that perhaps they were the ones who were in the wrong.

Life on the Island continued on in that way for many a long year. Every Sunday nayvogues used to come north from the parish of Ventry, from Dunquin and south from Ballincolla Pier and Coosnanay, and they would stay dancing there almost until dawn. Those nayvogues contained both girls and boys because the island boys wouldn't allow the visiting boys to take any island girl out dancing. That situation, however, was short-lived because the island boys came to prefer the foreign breed to the native one which was there for as long as people could remember. When they encountered the 'sheep' from the mainland I'm telling you they knocked sparks out of them as far as dancing was concerned. The island girls got the same treatment from the boys from the north. Even the old women were on the look-out to see if anyone might take them out dancing but they were very rarely invited. The young bird is the one, as the man from Crooked Cove said. Some of those people stuck by one another from the days of their youth until life's end because when they found a place that offered a living they married and spent a peaceful life together, but sadly that place was in a land across the sea.

A stranger with fluent Irish came with four children who were related to her. This lady's intention was to drum the spoken Irish of the island people into them. Those children used to go everywhere with the island children and they got to love one another. When this old lady told them one day that they would have to be getting ready for the journey home on the following day they didn't want to budge. Weren't they having the greatest of times under the sun, the strand and the hill, boats, swimming and the sea, and what could Dublin offer them only the flagstones on the streets and the noise and the din of the city? She was well able to control them and brought them back home again with twice as much Irish as they had when they came.

During holiday-time the following summer this lady together with the four children arrived on the Island again. Each of the four was by now acquainted with the life of the islanders and I promise you they weren't much sought after by the grown-ups, particularly the fishermen, because those children used to hop into the nayvogues faster than themselves and you could never tell when one of them might fall into the sea or have a crab stuck in his leg. Nevertheless the islanders were very kind to them because they were well-reared and mannerly.

On this her second visit the lady invited the local children and any others interested to listen to some music. They thought the night would never come. As they say, time passes slowly for those who wait. The night finally came and all the islanders big and small gathered. One of the girls from the visiting group got her box and placed it on the table. She opened it out and got it ready to play. Believe me she was able to play. There wasn't a sound or a peep out of anyone as they kept their eyes on the box and listened to the most beautiful music from it. Some of the old women and old men weren't too happy because they felt it was something miraculous and the sooner it was got rid of the better. The young boys and girls began to dance to the music and that was the lovely pleasant music. They continued on like that until bed-time. That is when the lady from Dublin announced that they had enough. 'Next Sunday,' she said, 'we'll have more music out on the road after Mass.'

That was the first gramophone ever to come to the Island and it aroused more interest than any other musical instrument that ever came since. That night it was christened 'Máire's Gramophone' and is still known as such by those who were there at the time.

Sunday came and the gramophone was brought out on to the road. The whole village gathered around it and the day was so beautiful that it could be heard back in Coumeenole. There were more than twenty donkeys on the Island in those days. Some of them were above on the side of the hill while the others were very close to where the gramophone was. When the gramophone bawled out its music a donkey bawled too. Then another donkey bawled and soon every donkey in the place was bawling. They went mad and it was impossible to hear the gramophone. The Dublin group preferred to listen to the donkeys than to the gramophone because they had never before seen donkeys going mad. Four of the donkeys got stuck in one another and everyone thought that they would let go at some stage, but not so. They never stopped until they toppled one another over the cliff. On seeing what had happened to the donkeys the people very nearly made two halves of the gramophone and of Máire as well. Never again was it brought outdoors. There was a lot of talk among the islanders about the gramophone as they were angered at what it had done to the four donkeys. Some old women later said that the devil himself was in it and was providing it with all its power because in their view nothing that was good ever did any harm.

The day came when Máire and her gramophone took their leave with no good wishes from those whose donkeys had fallen over the cliff. For as long as people inhabited the Island there was a saying there: 'Máire's gramophone and Seán's and Pad's donkeys.' There were some houses in the village where neither dancing nor music was afterwards allowed, not even if they were to be paid a fortune for it.

A young girl returned home from America and didn't she bring a gramophone with her! She placed it on the table one night and was just about to start playing it when her mother who was in the corner by the fire took up the tongs. She warned the girl to get the damned thing out of her house or else it would drive every cow and donkey in the village over the cliff. The girl didn't want to say anything but at dawn next day she packed her bags and headed northwards again. She has never since been seen or heard of.

One fine summer's morning some time later a boat arrived from England. She dropped anchor because she had come to buy lobsters, and had to wait until evening for the fishermen to come home. The captain took out his gramophone and began to play. There was twice as much music coming out of it as there was out of Máire's. Immediately the donkeys began bawling again but upon my soul if they did a man rounded them up and stabled them. It was the luck of God that he did so because they would have got stuck into one another again and maybe half of them might have gone over the cliff. The boat's captain got much more satisfaction out of the donkeys' music than out of that of the gramophone.

The people have now abandoned the Western Island until, as the man said, Tibb's Eve, and from the day they left neither music nor musical instruments matter a damn. The nicest sound anywhere is that of children and people and lonely is the place that is without those same two sounds. If anyone who knew the Island in its heyday were to pay a visit there today it would remind him of nothing but a large graveyard.

The day will yet come when there will be no point in telling people that such a life as I have described existed there for many years. When living on the Island I saw with my own two eyes the finest life I ever saw since and I'm very much afraid that I'll never again see the like of it.

Pádraig Tyers talking to Seán Ó Criomhthain

T: Seán, when did Carl Marstrander pay his first ever visit to the Island?

Ó C: As far as I can recall Carl Marstrander came to the Island in the year 1909, and he was nearly one of the first strangers or visitors ever to come there. Only one or two others had come before him and they didn't remain very long. As far as I know and remember Cormac Ó Cadhlaigh was the first stranger I ever saw on the Blaskets. I can't say where he was from. Some say he was from Killorglin, others say from Dublin. He was a wonderful man where Irish was concerned and all he wanted was to be listening to the people of the Blaskets talking and conversing with one another.

He already knew a great deal about Tomás Ó Criomhthain because Tomás used to write in Irish and Cormac had read his writings. That was his reason for coming to the Blaskets. He spent some time in the company of the people talking and chatting and singing and dancing and gossiping with them and he got the devil's own enjoyment out of it. He got plenty of Irish too though he had already quite a good command of it. However the day came when he said goodbye to the Blasket and went off. After coming to the Island Marstrander stayed there for almost six months.

T: Did he have Irish at that time?

Ó C: He had a smattering of it but he wasn't really fluent. He was able to read and write and understand it, wherever he learned it. The islanders didn't know where he got it but he himself said he learned it in England.

T: Where was he working at that time?

Ó C: That I cannot say, but he was living in Norway and I don't know what he was doing there. I never heard anything in that regard, unless he was working in a museum or some place.

T: Who first drew his attention to this part of the country?

Ó C: Bláithín did. You know yourself who Bláithín was, Robin Flower. He worked in the British Museum where he was nearly the top man. He too had a smattering of Irish at that time and could read it. He said to Marstrander: 'To find the only place

with real living Irish you must go as far west as possible.'
Bláithín didn't mention Dunquin or the Island or anything else,
just simply 'as far west as possible'. He didn't need to give much
advice to Marstrander because Marstrander was well able to
recognise the real living language.

T: How was it that Marstrander was advised to go to the
Island rather than somewhere else?

Ó C: As soon as he reached Dingle he began to make enquiries and found out that an islander named Ó Catháin lived in
the town. Ó Catháin was a relative of our own. He told Marstrander that the living Irish was to the west and that the best
place for him to go was west and if he could to go to the Blasket.
Marstrander then enquired of the man if there was anyone there
who could read and write Irish and was also a native speaker. 'I
can't say,' said the Dingle man, 'if they can write it but they certainly can speak it.'

'Right,' said Marstrander, 'I'll go as far as Dunquin.'

He left Dingle and his next stop was in Ballyferriter. A man
from the village advised him to remain in Ballyferriter as there
were people there who were fluent native speakers of Irish.

'Furthermore,' said the Ballyferriter man, 'there's not much
sense in going into the Island and drowning yourself.'

Marstrander made no reply but it wasn't long until he heard
English being spoken by somebody to one side or the other of
him. He was talking to this man in a public house. 'Yes,' he said,
'my enemy is just behind my ear.' He later told Tomás about this.

At that time the Island postman used to go out to Dunquin
every Tuesday and Friday, and Marstrander found out that if he
was in Dunquin on the following Tuesday he could travel free
to the Island, so he went to Dunquin where he met the postman
and made arrangements with him to go in. He also got lodgings
in the postman's house. That man was the King. They set off and
Marstrander was delighted. They reached the Island and Marstrander got out of the nayvogue on to the pier. He was a strong,
hardy and athletic man over six feet in height and had little
spare flesh on him but he was as healthy as a salmon. He went
to the King's house and stayed there. Next day he went around
the village and had a look around. He asked the King endless
questions and the King sent him to my father who he knew

could read and write Irish. He also told Marstrander that if my father couldn't fill the bill there was nothing more he himself could do.

Marstrander and my father got together and it so happened that Marstrander was pleased with the old man. Tomás was fishing in those days and had no time to spend with Marstrander during the day but he used to drop into him about seven o'clock in the evening. They would go back to the room and Tomás would stay with the Norseman – that is the name by which he was then known to the islanders – from seven until ten. That was the night session and they would spend the time talking and reading and writing Irish. That was their routine. Marstrander carried on until he and Tomás had spent five months working together, but before the fifth month had passed word had come to Marstrander that he must return home as those who were replacing him at work were finding the going tough. What did he do then but ask Tomás to give him two sessions, one in the morning and one in the afternoon. I imagine Tomás was tired, exhausted and fed up of the work but he did not like to refuse him. 'We'll manage,' he said, 'I won't refuse you.' So he and the Norseman decided on two sessions a day for a fortnight, and when that was over Marstrander had to bid goodbye to the place and leave. He and Tomás completed their term together and they were both very grateful to one another. Marstrander was a generous man.

When around the place by day he used to teach the young boys a lot of athletics, jumping and so on, and they were mad about him. He was a man who had the world of athletic skills. He would catch hold of a nayvogue mast, make a dash, take a running jump, stick the end of the mast into the ground and rise as high as the tops of the houses. The old women used to say: 'Oh the poor man, he'll kill himself. He's mad!'

He would get five or six boys to hold hands. Then he would jump on their hands saying: 'One, two. Throw me up when I say three.' They would throw him up in the air, he would turn belly-up and land on his back amongst them again.

T: He used to stay in the King's house?

Ó C: Yes, in the King's house. He and the King and the King's son Seán, God be good to them, were great friends. He settled in on the Blasket and spent twenty-one weeks there speaking nothing whatsoever but Irish, but I was young then and didn't take any interest in their conversations. After returning home Marstrander used to write to Tomás giving him all the news and Tomás used to write back. I remember that after he went home he sent big long pages to Tomás and asked him to make a list of the names of all the birds around the Blaskets, how many eggs they had in their nests, how many chicks were born to them and so on. Tomás spent up to a year writing in detail to Marstrander but I don't know what happened to Marstrander's work, or what became of it.

T: Did he pay any further visits before his death?

Ó C: He didn't visit the Island but he came to Dublin where he was talking to some man from the Folklore Commission. I think it was Ó Duilearga.* He remarked to Ó Duilearga: 'If I could find a boat which would bring me to Dunquin or the Blasket and back again I'd go there.' He didn't, however, wish to come to stay there. I imagine he lived to be very old.

After returning from the Island to England he called to Bláithín at the British Museum and informed him that he had just been in the best schoolroom for learning Irish, that he had tried Ventry, Dingle and the Parish O'Moore and other places but he wasn't happy with the Irish in any place until he met and spoke with the old people on the Blaskets. Having heard Marstrander's story Bláithín himself packed his bags the following year and didn't stop nor stay until he reached the Blasket. He was given a room by the King and his daughter Cáit an Rí, a woman who, the Lord have mercy on the dead, was well able to look after him and give him plenty of Irish. He asked Cáit where Marstrander's teacher lived.

'If you looked out the window,' said Cáit an Rí, 'you could see the top of his chimney below the bank.'

'I must call to him,' he said.

He called to Tomás and he and Tomás spent many years talking, writing and gossiping. There wasn't a thing in Tomás' head that he didn't drag out of it. He also called to Peig Sayers and all the old women on the Blaskets, to Méiní Céitinn and Gobnait Ní Chinnéide and everyone who had anything to contribute. He continued to come to the Blaskets, himself and his wife and children, until finally his health failed and on his deathbed he arranged that his ashes be scattered on the hill on the Island. His wish was carried out. The ashes are there to this day if only they could be seen. That was the end of Bláithín.

T: That was the name given to Robin Flower by the people of the Blasket?

Ó C: Yes, that was the name given to Robin Flower by the people of the Blasket, so it was. After Bláithín and Marstrander and Ó Cadhlaigh had spent periods on the Island other visitors came from Dublin and Cork and even Limerick. They were looking for somewhere to stay but there were no suitable houses on the Blasket then, but a couple of houses were found for them and soon six visitors arrived. Their knowledge of Irish was poor but they had their ears cocked listening to the poor wretches, the fools as the locals described themselves, and they were very pleased. They had dancing and music and fresh fish and every sort of sea-food to munch so that they felt they were in heaven. Their numbers were increasing each year according as they could get places to stay. Religious brothers and priests started coming, among them a priest from County Clare, Seoirse Mac Clúin. He set to work on the book called *Réilthíní Óir*. He had lists of words on paper for everyone and would ask people to put them into sentences, and I guarantee you that the islanders and the schoolchildren were busily engaged going to the old people to collect words for Seoirse. He was always known as Seoirse.

Another Seoirse or George later arrived, George Thomson, the man mainly responsible for Muiris Ó Súilleabháin's book, *Twenty Years A-Growing*. George's command of Irish was better than that of Muiris or anybody else among us and he made a great job of Muiris' book. He produced an Irish version and an English version, both of them well done. He proved himself a real gentleman by his work on behalf of the islanders and the assistance which he gave them.

***

T: Seán, I see your pipe there on the hob.

Ó C: It is there all right. A tough enough pipe.

T: Is that so?

Ó C: There's nothing surer.

T: What age were you, if you remember, when you started smoking?

Ó C: Well, I'll give you a good idea of my age then, about seven years.

T: When you started?

Ó C: When I started. And I'll tell you something else. I had a little jacket with a pocket on the outside near the oxter, and if you ever saw a crab's windpipe.

T: No, I didn't.

Ó C: A crab has large claws and a large finger. If properly cleaned it would take a half-ounce of tobacco. You would remove a little piece from the tip and there's a hole going right through it. You would put the tobacco carefully into that and place it beside the fire. Then you would get the tongs, shove an ember down into it, put it into your mouth and smoke away. We used to have one of those in our pockets going to school, my man, and tobacco which we had stolen! That tobacco wasn't given to us. We stole it during the night or during the day. If you found that your grandfather had taken off his trousers and was asleep you tried it to see if it contained any tobacco. It usually did, so you gave it the knife and put it into your pocket.

T: But was this crab's pipe the first pipe you ever had?

Ó C: It was and we had it a good while, for the four or five years we spent in school. If we were seen with a pipe during our school-days and found to have tobacco on us we were given the stick. We were, my boy, or if we didn't get the stick we got a real lashing of the tongue.

T: Where used you smoke at first when you didn't have your parents' permission?

Ó C: There was an old man who had a house which we called Pad's house. He lived there on his own and was getting on in years. We used to do odd jobs for him whenever he asked us, a load of turf and other things from the hill. He always had a blazing red fire and four or five of us tricksters or playboys used to call in there after school. Each of us would have a clay pipe in his mouth sending smoke around the house and up the chimney. That was where we smoked our tobacco and it often turned us backsides up because it used to affect us. The tobacco in those days was very strong, not like today's. You would vomit then and when you went home the grandmother would ask what caused you to be so pale. She knew only too well that we had got the tobacco somewhere. When pipes were given out at wakes a young lad would often pick up the full pipe which his father or mother had brought home, scoop a fistful of the tobacco out of its bowl, and hide it in a hole in a fence so that we would have it to smoke in Pad's house later on.

T: Do you remember smoking for the first time in the presence of your parents?

Ó C: I never smoked in the presence of my parents until I left school. No, never. My father had a pipe at that time and he used to put it aside on the hob. No sooner would he do so than I would light the pipe again and send a fog of tobacco up all over the house. 'You're starting good and early,' he would remark.

T: What about the women? They also had a liking for tobacco?

Ó C: Some of them. There were three or four women, I would say, on the Island and they were better than any man at polishing off tobacco, so they were.

T: Did each one of them have her own plug of tobacco?

Ó C: They had none of their own but when the man of the house was around he would cut a piece of tobacco and leave it aside and if that much didn't do her she would have to wait until he came back. He would fill the pipe for her and leave her a little bit extra because he would have to take the remainder away in his pocket going back up the hill or to sea or some other damned place. If the woman who smoked didn't have enough tobacco, do you understand, she could go up to Cáit and get a puff from her until her own pipe was filled again.

T: They took every second turn?

Ó C: They took the stump, the short-stemmed pipe, in turns.

T: You mentioned the sea a few moments ago. Did the fishermen smoke at sea?

Ó C: Oh, they smoked a lot at sea. It's a great place for smoking. Some nights, however, if you were catching fish you would not get the opportunity to smoke because your hands would be wet and if they were wet you couldn't redden the pipe, you see.

The water would get into it.

T: Were there superstitions connected with smoking at sea?

Ó C: There were at times. If you were searching for fish during the night and you happened to come across some where you were searching while the other boats were some distance away or searching for fish also, in that case when you sensed there were fish in the net you would have to cover yourself. You were not allowed to light a match in the open.

T: What do you mean by covering yourself?

Ó C: You put the oilcoat down over your head and got down into the bottom of the nayvogue. Perhaps one of the other men might throw an old sack down on top of you so that the light couldn't be seen, do you understand? In that case the light couldn't be seen by the fish because you had to strike the match on the boat-seat, but then some fellow in another boat would see the light and say: 'There's another boat still out and there must be a reason for it. They're catching something.'

T: So it was easy to see the light?

Ó C: It was indeed. On a dark night at sea if any red flame rises up you'll see it, so you will. If you're at sea at night and a boat is sailing along you can see it miles and miles away from you.

T: Did the islanders use much snuff?

Ó C: Those old women who didn't smoke used it, but the women who smoked didn't need much snuff and they didn't have it either.

T: By the way was there any shop on the Island where one could buy tobacco and other things?

Ó C: There was never any shop on the Island. Not even sweets were sold there. The only thing I ever saw for sale there was that thing called the Bandon Rattler, whatever sort of thing it was.

T: Was it porter or cider?

Ó C: It was porter that used to come up from Cork. There were people locally who used to send barrels of it in for sale. If you went to Dingle you would get two barrels from a publican. 'Bring those two barrels west and if you bring any money back to me ...' You got a penny for yourself for every pint you sold. I think that a barrel of porter in those days cost twenty-one shillings. Some of those who brought it in kept it for their own use while others sold it. But some smart fellow came along then and began sending so many barrels in for sale each week. That is when life on the Island was at its best.

T: By the way how many people were there on the Island when you were growing up?

Ó C: Indeed I suppose there were nearly two hundred, so there were.

T: At what age did the young people usually start drinking in the presence of their parents?

Ó C: No matter what age you were if you were fishing and earning and had some money of your own there was no objection. You'd be fishing there at fifteen years of age, so you would.

T: Did they bring drink home from this shop, this speak-easy you mentioned?

Ó C: The old people brought it home but not the young people or adults. The adults used to go to the houses where the drink was on sale because, you understand, they had their own company and pastime there. They discussed matters relating to fishing and lobsters and hillwork and sheep and animals and so on, and if you needed to go out to Dunquin some morning with an animal or a cow or some such thing you'd get others who also had business to attend to outside. You'd ask: 'Have you any business outside tomorrow or do you want to go out? I'm bringing something out myself.' Or you might say: 'I'm going out tomorrow with five or six sheep.' You arranged matters in this way. Another man might say that he intended going out too, that he might as well do that as stay at home. They helped one another out in that way.

T: Did they drink much? Would you ever see anyone drunk?

Ó C: I never saw anyone drunk there, never. You might see a fellow getting a stagger here and there but that was far from being drunk. As a man once said: 'I never saw a fellow sitting on his backside due to drink.' No, never.

T: You mentioned that boys of fifteen years of age were fishing and earning. Did they have any pastimes?

Ó C: One pastime we had was carpentry which we used to do in the outhouses at night-time. We had chisels and saws and awls for making chairs and tables and presses and so on at night-time and on wet evenings. One man might be making a little nayvogue, another a press and another a dresser.

T: They were learning from one another?

Ó C: Learning from one another and some of them were really tip top, so they were.

T: Tomás was very good at that type of work, wasn't he?

Ó C: I imagine that it was Tomás who taught them all the trade. He was a tradesman. He'd begin with the stone. He'd make the windows, put the roof on the house and tie it down. He'd plaster it and do everything except turn the key in the door.

T: Where did he get the timber to make the windows?

Ó C: It all came from the sea. There was timber to be got at sea in those days from which windows were made, I might say, for the past eighty years and those windows still haven't rotted. They called it red deal. Tomás also did some tailoring and the women used to come to him. You know those white flannel garments. Some of those women couldn't cut a drawers or a waistcoat for their men to wear and so they would come to Tomás. He had a pattern and he'd cut out the drawers and waistcoat for them. He was skilled in another way too, in making baskets and panniers, if you ever heard of them. He could make tackling for a donkey, the mat, the straddle and the pannier. He also made the pannier-bottoms and skillets and withes and tightened the whole pannier together so that you had nothing to do but take it and put it on the donkey and then you were ready for the hill. Everyone in the village was after him saying 'Make a basket for me,' or 'I must make a pannier.' He refused nobody. During the winter when he had the opportunity he could make two panniers a day, and making panniers is no joke. You need skill and good training to make them and, as the man said, to make tackling for a donkey.

T: Was he by any chance able to weave?

Ó C: He was because there was a woman out in Dunquin, a sister to his brother's wife, and he used to stay in her house any time he was on the mainland. She was a weaver and he learned the craft from her. He learned it from another man also, Seán Ó Criomhthain, who lived up in Vicarstown. He was known as

Seán Glas. Tomás often stayed in his house and did some weaving with him.

T: Did the young lads have any other pastimes, hunting rabbits or something like that?

Ó C: I wouldn't consider hunting rabbits a pastime. It is the very opposite in fact. It is hard laborious work. I don't remember them having any pastime except on a wet night in a house where there would be music and girls. The old people loved dancing and music and seeing young boys and girls enjoying themselves.

T: What did ye catch rabbits?

Ó C: We had slings to catch them, as you might say. Other people call them snares but we always called them slings.

T: How were they made?

Ó C: You may remember that copper wire which used to be available in large very light skeins long ago. You'd make a sling on two little sticks. It was a foot and a half to two feet high. You put two loops on it and wove it nice and neatly so that it was very strong. You put one loop through the other and that was it. You'd then get a nice bit of cord and attach a stake to one end of it. After that you looked for a rabbit's track just like the crease on your trouser. 'There's the path,' one man would say to another. 'There's a rabbit using that,' because a rabbit always follows the same path. He's liable to come out of his burrow on the western or the eastern side. You'd drive the stake into the ground and set the sling the height of your fist above the grass, and you can be sure that whether he came from the west or from the east the sling would choke him, though not completely unless there was a fall of ground where he might topple over and couldn't run. In that case he was hanged.

T: What kept the slings standing?

Ó C: Oh, what used they call it? Oh yes, it was known as a stander. I don't know the Irish for it. It was a small stick not nearly as thick as the stake, in fact not half as thick. You just stuck the tip of it into the ground, pressed the sling into it and left it in that position until morning. You'd come home then tired out from walking the hill because you had to go a long distance from the house in search of paths up and down the hill. You had to be up again before daybreak, head for the place where you set the first

99

snare and start to search around. The day might have dawned by the time you reached the last of them and maybe you might have lost two fine rabbits to the black-backed gull and the common gull. The black-backed gull is a devil if ever there was one.

T: She'd kill the rabbit if he was alive?

Ó C: She wouldn't think twice about it. Wouldn't she pick the two eyes out of his head! And, do you know, the rabbit is an animal that's no good to fight anything at all because he dies with fright. He gets a heart attack or some damned thing.

T: Of course rabbits were plentiful on the Island?

Ó C: They were indeed, as plentiful as ferns. They're still there, millions of them.

T: Used ye eat them?

Ó C: We used indeed, and you never tasted anything like them in the morning when they were fried with a couple of slices of bacon under them. To hear them frying in the oven would make your teeth water. The old women had great big ovens in those days in which they used to fry five or six rabbits that crackled on a red hot fire with onions and pepper and the bacon underneath. Yerrah, any rabbit that wasn't too old was lovely, just like chicken. It was even better than chicken. We could easily tell if a rabbit was fairly old, even when skinning him.

T: How could you tell?

Ó C: Because when you catch a young rabbit and skin him and take the two hind legs off him the skin will come off straightaway with one pull because he's young. But it won't come off the old stager, just like an old man! It will remain stuck to him. Such a rabbit was called an old buck, you understand, an old buck rabbit.

T: A buck?

Ó C: Yes, a buck. They often threw those old ones away, that is the ones that were too long on the go and had nothing to do but make out for themselves. Those were salted and islanders who had relatives in Dunquin or maybe north in the parish of Ballyferriter or the parish of Ventry would dry them and put them into sacks – they would have already been tanned and cured – and bring them out to those relatives pretending that they were really good rabbits. The islanders were always smart, you know. The people on the mainland found nothing wrong with those rabbits. All they wanted was meat. They would cut them up into pieces or, as you might say, quarter them. They would get half a pig's head and put the half-head and the rabbits together into one pot and you had soup the like of which you never tasted. The flavour of the bacon went right through it and if the whole lot was put on the table you would go for the old rabbit sooner than the half-head. You would indeed.

T: The old rabbit was called a buck?

Ó C: He was.

T: And what was a young rabbit called?

Ó C: A young rabbit was known as a leveret, one that would have just been born and you'd see him running in and out of the burrow. When a month or two old he was known as a half-grown rabbit. He's really like chicken because he's young. A leveret, a half-grown rabbit and an old buck, and the other was the doe.

T: I see. What did ye do with the skin?

Ó C: When the skins were taken off you'd put them outdoors if the sun was shining. You'd leave them for a full day in the sun. You had to bring them in then, get a string and put it through the eyes in the skin. You hung all the skins beside one another from the beams near the mantelpiece over the fire to harden them. They became as hard as a piece of timber and stayed that way. You then gathered them and sent them through the post three dozen at a time. The post wouldn't take any more. You parcelled the three dozen together and sent them to Cork or Dublin where there were firms that bought them. If they were in good condition you might get three shillings for them. Those with black patches on them were not first grade but the bright skins that had no black patches would make four shillings a dozen. The buyers covered the postal charges which were shown on the cheque that you received. That's how it was done.

T: Where were they sent? To England?

Ó C: The people of the Blaskets sent them to Dublin or Cork, but I cannot say what was done with them afterwards. There you have it, boy.

T: By the way were there any hares on the Island?

Ó C: I never saw a hare on the Island. We didn't have such

an animal, but I did hear of a man from Dingle who sent two hares to the island called Beginis just off the Blasket. I suppose he knew what he was doing but the plan wasn't successful because they failed to breed there. They were sent to Inisvickillane but they didn't breed there either. There was no stoat on the Blasket nor any of those things called frogs. We didn't have the like. There were neither stoats nor frogs nor hares there.

T: Did ye have any rats?

Ó C: Nor any rats either. No, but there were mice. I suppose that there are many other animals too which we didn't have but I just can't remember them. But I know for certain that we had mice and that they are still there, so they are.

T: Of course mice are harmless creatures.

Ó C: Oh they're certainly harmless to people but they used to damage the grain and the oats and the corn of the islanders. They'd get into the stack and if you didn't remake the stack they wouldn't leave you a grain. They'd make a hole in it and burrow down into the ground. Then they'd bring the grain down into that hole, come up again and eat away. I often saw a stack, if you could call it that, being knocked for remaking with maybe forty mice in it, and dogs and bitches and cats tearing them from one another. I did indeed.

There was a man I knew and I remember seeing him giving a sheaf of oats to the cow in wintertime. He'd hit the head of the sheaf off a barrel which he had close by and a good amount of the grain would fall down into the barrel. He was collecting the grain to give to the donkey during the spring. He'd then throw the sheaf to the cow. He noticed, however, that the level of grain in the barrel wasn't rising in spite of the amount he was threshing and he wondered why. He put his hand down into the barrel. There was nothing in it but chaff. He got a large globe, the kind used on lamps long ago, with a big belly on it and a wide mouth. He then got a cork and stuck it up into the lower end leaving the mouth on top open. He stuck the globe down into the oats, dropped about a quarter of a pound of threshed oats into it and placed a little board across the mouth. Every single mouse that climbed up on the board jumped down into the globe. Because the globe was so smooth there wasn't a hope that the mice could climb back to the top. When the man examined the globe next morning it had turned grey in colour. It was full to the brim of mice. He put one hand on the top of the globe and the other under the cork and brought it outdoors. There was a large barrel of water outside the house. He turned the globe upside down and in that one go he drowned seventeen mice.

T: Since there wasn't, or rather isn't, any river on the Island I presume that there were no otters there either?

Ó C: Indeed, boy, that's not so at all. They were very plentiful. There are places on the Island named after the otter, such as the Otter's Foreshore and so on. There are large foreshores into which these otters go just as the seals do.

T: In the salt water?

Ó C: They go in under the rocks and the stones and make caves there.

T: How many days a week used the islanders fish?

Ó C: Six days a week when fishing for lobsters and five days a week for mackerel because there was no market at the week-end. If you went out fishing on Saturdays nobody would buy it on Sundays, and that's why they didn't fish on Saturday nights.

T: The fish had to be brought out to Dunquin?

Ó C: It had. After a night's fishing you carried your sack containing a hundredweight of fish on top of your head up the Great Cliff, if you know where that is. Maybe you do.

T: Yes, I do, to the west of Dunquin.

Ó C: That's where it is. You had to walk up to the top, then come back home and spend the whole night fishing. You might get two thousand mackerel and the crew of three would have to carry the whole lot up the cliff and be back again on the Island about two or three o'clock.

T: Ye used to bring the fish out every night?

Ó C: We used, but not unless the night was very fine, because you couldn't tell what the tide might be like with the nayvogue too deep in the water. You had to wait until daybreak or near it anyway.

T: In wintertime when there was no fishing due to bad weather what time would ye get up in the morning?

Ó C: About ten o'clock, but somebody in the house would have to be up before nine. The ass would be below in the room bawling non-stop and the cow roaring. If she happened to have a drop of milk you had to milk her and give her a few potatoes. After doing that you'd go up the hill. There were always big clamps of turf covered inside a stone structure and as dry as a bean, and yourself and the donkey would bring that home during the winter. If you didn't there might be the odd thief, maybe your neighbour, you understand, who would come along and have a go at it!

T: Why didn't ye bring home all the turf at the one time during the summer?

Ó C: You couldn't bring anything home at the one time when you had only a donkey. Each man had his own donkey. There were often twenty donkeys ahead of us going back the hill in the morning and you'd see one donkey snapping at another and sending its pannier and tackling up in the air. You'd have to run after him for fear the pannier might disappear down over the cliff, so you would.

T: Tell me about the Dingle fair, Seán.

Ó C: I remember well the fair day coming, especially the November fair which was the most important one of all for the islanders because by that time every beast was fine and fat and well worth bringing to market. You'd go up the hill on Friday morning – Saturday was fair day – and go running after sheep. You had enough to do by the time you caught about twenty sheep or so, put them into a boat or nayvogue in Goods Strand, bring them out to Dunquin, and let them off up onto the road tied together in twos with a rope. That rope had to be sound because if it broke even the peelers couldn't catch up with the two that got away. Off you went into Dingle, twelve or maybe thirteen miles of road, and by the time you got to Dingle neither yourself nor the sheep were worth the ten of clubs. The butcher came along and you had to let him have them for whatever price he was prepared to give because there was no question of bringing them home again. It was the same with the man who had a cow or a beast for sale. He had to bring her down to the slip, knock her, tie her and put her into the nayvogue. To do so required the assistance of six tough strong able men who knew their job.

T: How did ye tie the cattle?

Ó C: They had to be knocked to the ground and their four legs tied together. You also needed to know how to tie them and the rope had to be sound. Then they were put into the nayvogue and if you noticed the legs working loose you put the bale – there was one in every nayvogue to bale her – into the water and poured a couple of balefuls on the rope. That tightened the ropes effectively. When you got to the slip at the Great Cliff the slip might be too high and in that case you had to run the nayvogue in on the gravel on some little stony-bottomed rocky spot, tilt the nayvogue over on one gunwale and haul the cattle out. The gunwale was often broken in the process. Up you'd go then to the Great Cliff, a difficult passage at that time, and from there to Dingle fair. Some islanders used to put them into some field until morning while others who didn't bother doing so sold them straightaway and had to accept whatever price they were offered. You spent that night in Dingle. You'd have a drink and when that went down you felt as happy as if you never had a poor relative. There were songs and chat and fellows were often at one another's throats. One man might get a wallop from another fellow and they would rake up memories and deeds of other days and so on. Then they departed for home and on their return to the Island they were as happy as the President of the United States. Next day every one of them went off again about his business, so he did.

T: They never brought the cattle or the sheep back home from the fair, I suppose.

Ó C: There was no chance of that. You had to be satisfied with the price you got. The Island isn't like the mainland, you understand, because you can't bring them home and wait for another fair. Whatever you got for your stock you had to accept it. That was the way with the fair. The women always accompanied the men, and only for the women I suppose some of the men mightn't return for three months because the people of the Blaskets were the devils for drink when they could lay hands on it.

T: Did they keep many cattle in those days?

Ó C: The head of each household had just one beast and quite often that beast wouldn't be ready at all within the year. He'd have to wait until the following year and by that time it might be two years old. There was a man in Dingle who had an island called Beginis – it was one of the Blaskets – and he used to buy a lot of cattle and put them grazing on Beginis so as to have them ready for the following year. He bought a lot of cattle from the islanders and that brought them great relief in the end.

T: Nobody had a second animal?

Ó C: No, but some of them might have two cows in summertime to provide milk for visitors but with the coming of winter they would get rid of them. Every farmer had just a cow, a calf and a donkey.

T: What crops did ye grow on the Island?

Ó C: Potatoes and oats. I never saw any other crops there. An odd person might grow a handful of onions. That was all.

T: Was the land able to produce those crops?

Ó C: It was indeed, and during the war when the flour was scarce some man or other sowed a patch of wheat and it cropped very well.

T: I suppose that sometimes in the depth of winter there were problems with food supplies.

Ó C: There were. Food didn't last long in houses where there were large families, but if those families were in trouble other houses came to their rescue. They would seek help from the house where there was only the husband and wife and maybe a third person and that help was provided until food became plentiful again. Then when a fine day would come and you'd see all the food they brought home in the nayvogue you'd think a ship had arrived in port, flour and meal and tea and sugar. The shortage of tobacco I think affected them most of all. Some of them would rather fast for a couple of days than be without a smoke.

T: What did ye do when the supply of flour failed?

Ó C: When that happened they had to turn to the potatoes, so they had.

T: Three times a day?

Ó C: Three times a day. That seldom happened, however, because they always had yellow meal for the cows and when the flour ran out, you see, they baked a yellow meal cake that was like a flagstone.

T: I suppose that sometimes they were unable to come out to the mainland for a couple of weeks.

Ó C: Indeed they were.

T: Well what happened if a person became ill during that time?

Ó C: If someone became ill you'd make a dash to bring in the doctor. That was their greatest problem. They'd leave no stone unturned if a young person became ill and needed a doctor. Four men would hop into a nayvogue but the doctor never liked coming back to the Island with them. The weather wasn't always suitable, yet he'd come and when it wasn't suitable he'd tell them to leave him on the Island. He'd prefer to stay anywhere on the Island rather than face the return sea journey. Quite often when a priest came in on a bad day he'd stay there too, something that wasn't really necessary, I'd say.

T: Seán, how often did the mail-boat make the journey out to Dunquin?

Ó C: The mail-boat went out to Dunquin twice a week on Tuesdays and Fridays and people would go out there with the postman to get messages. On their return the whole village, at least those who were free, would gather at the edge of the pier where the postman always opened his bag and distributed the letters and parcels and everything else. He even sold them stamps. They'd then question him about this and that, and if he had any bad news they didn't like hearing it. I remember well the time of the Easter Rising in Dublin when the islanders had relatives living there. They became very worried on hearing about Dublin being on fire and about the soldiers and the fighting and so on. And then again when France was involved in the Great War the poor fishermen were very upset because there was nobody coming to buy the lobsters from them except the French. I'm telling you that what was happening on the mainland worried all who were in their right minds, if indeed they were in their right minds, because they got a hard time of it from the world and from life. People also had a worrying time during the Second Great War when the Yanks came over because some of them had children and their children's children fighting in the war.

T: Talking of the mail-boat, where did the letters usually come from?

Ó C: They came from Ballyferriter.

T: No, I mean who used to write to the people on the Island?

Ó C: Oh, to the people of the Island. Most of the letters came from the United States and a very odd one from England. Many is the letter and other things that came to the Blaskets from Bláithín and George Thomson, while lots of parcels came by post from shopkeepers in Dublin. I remember five and six pound parcels of tea coming to the Blaskets from those Dublin shop-keepers. You'd send for a certain amount of tea and it used to come packed grand and tight. Would you believe the price of tea in those days? Five pounds of it for a half-sovereign down from Becker Brothers. The children used to be throwing the parcels up in the air all around the village.

T: It was more convenient to buy it like that than to go into Dingle for it?

Ó C: It was indeed, more convenient. Later on it became very convenient, you understand. Maybe you heard of that well-known man from Ballyferriter, Liam Ó Lúing. He was known as 'Irish Liam' and carried a card on his chest that read 'Speak Irish to me.' He used to go to the Island and always took a notebook with him. 'What do you want?' 'Such and such a thing.' 'And what else and what else and what else?' and 'Write it down.' He'd write it down and then take his note-book with him. There was this particular house in Dunquin, Máire Céitinn's, and he'd send a boy south with a horse and cart and the goods would be kept in Máire's house. The islanders would come out for whatever they wanted and within a fortnight the credit given by Liam would have run out. He'd then go back again to Máire's with his note-book. 'Pay me, pay me! The credit is up!' he'd say. 'Pay me! There's more due to me!' He was very good to them, so he was.

T: I presume that the men went to Dingle from time to time and could do their own shopping, but what about the women?

Ó C: Well, some of the men from the Island who used to go to Dingle were wonderful but there were others who used to go there and they weren't worth sending. The women would have to accompany them and of course the men would rather they didn't. The women would have to go there to buy clothes for the family and they kept great control over the men who hated the idea of the women going to Dingle.

T: How often did the women go there?

Ó C: There were women on the Island who never went to Dingle but there were some who went there every week, others once every three months and others once a year. They used to wait for letters and relief to come from America and when the dollars came they knocked sparks out of them. They'd often buy boots. There were men on the Island who never allowed their wives to go to Dingle. They did everything themselves. They'd get little written notes from their wives, my dear man, put those notes into their pockets, and call into a woman in Dingle who was well-known to them. She'd put everything into a box for them and tie it up.

T: But in the case of such a man what happened if his wife needed a coat – well she wouldn't need a coat – but boots for example?

Ó C: Boots?

T: Yes. How would he know what size to get?

Ó C: He knew the size very well because the woman in the shop knew it.

T: I have another question for you, Seán.

Ó C: You're welcome, boy.

T: I was told that there's a place on the Island where only unbaptised children were buried. Is that true?

Ó C: If that's true, Pádraig, I'm not aware of it. And I'm certain sure and I know very well that there is no such place. But as you know there's a graveyard on the Island known as Castle Point Graveyard and children, whether baptised or not, and old people who died during a spell of bad weather are all buried there together. But there's no place where unbaptised children are buried.

T: I suppose it is years since people were buried in that graveyard.

Ó C: People were buried there during my own lifetime and people were buried there before my time. It was said, and it is true, that a woman was buried there at the time of the Spanish Armada. That's a long time ago but the grave is outside the boundary of the graveyard and is marked by stones at its head and foot. It is said that this woman was on the ship named the

Santa Maria or whatever you call it, and was found on the White Strand. She came ashore on the strand and was laden with gold rings, it seems. Her body was wrapped in sheets and sacks, and a hole was made for it and she's buried in Castle Point Graveyard.

T: A Spanish woman you say?

Ó C: A Spanish woman and they say she was on that ship.

T: Castle Point Graveyard, called after Piaras Feirtéar's castle?

Ó C: That's where Piaras had his castle. There's a large well inside it down in a glen and a fearsome cove near it on the other side.

T: Talking of Piaras Feirtéar, where on the Island did he have his cave?

Ó C: His cave was up to two miles from where he had his castle. You'd need to be as agile as a cat to get into the cave which was Piaras' hide-out. I was often in it, so I was. But talking of children a few minutes ago and where they were buried, I know of two sets of twins who were born on the Island in my own lifetime and died very soon after birth, and I saw those two sets of twins being carried by their parents in four little boxes and being buried in the graveyard where children who had been baptised and confirmed were also buried.

T: Why were some of the people buried there and not brought out to Dunquin graveyard?

Ó C: It wasn't possible because of bad weather. And, suppose if in the old days there was a person living alone on the Island the graveyard there was as suitable for him as any other one. In those old days most corpses were brought out so that first of all the priest could be present at the funeral and also that they could be buried in their ancestors' graveyard. All the islanders had their own ancestry and that ancestry was on the mainland and so they all wished to be brought out to the old family graveyard. There are graves in those old graveyards and if you examined some of them as I did you might notice that there were up to nine coffins on top of one another with the later ones covered with stones above ground level so that they allowed air and light and other things in.

T: You mentioned two sets of twins who were born on the

Island and died very soon afterwards. Was it for want of a doctor that they died so quickly?

Ó C: I can't say. Maybe if there were twenty-one doctors available they couldn't keep them alive. Then again maybe they could. But on an island you can't get a doctor at short notice. As for those two sets of twins both mothers were named Máire, would you believe, and there was much talk about the two Máires and their twins, the poor things, and what a great source of joy it would be if they survived after birth.

T: Were they the only twins born there?

Ó C: Oh no. Other twins were born there too before that, so they were. I'm telling you, boy, the islanders weren't idle!

***

T: Seán, how many in family did your father have?

Ó C: My father had a dozen in family.

T: And your mother died young, I understand.

Ó C: My mother died young in childbirth. She died giving birth and that left me the second last child. I don't remember ever having seen her. I don't even know what colour she was.

T: What sort of a man was your father in build and temperament?

Ó C: Oh he wasn't a tall man, but he was a strong well-built stocky fellow about thirteen stone in weight. A fine placid, gentle man who didn't like any fighting or quarrelling or bickering, and he was anxious that everything would be nice and civil. He often made peace between the neighbours and used to tell them that there was nothing worse than quarrelling.

T: So he was the kind of father that a young boy would like to have?

Ó C: Oh, I was delighted to have him as my father. Himself and myself used to have great fun when we were alone together.

T: I understand that he was able to read and write English from his childhood, something he couldn't do in Irish.

Ó C: He was. That's how it was, because no Irish was being taught in the Blasket School when Tomás was going there nor indeed after he left the school. Tomás was never shown how to write his name in Irish while he was at the Blasket School but he was a master at English, as they used to say, and the old people often described him as 'Dónall's Scholar' – Dónall was his father – because of his learning and knowledge of English.

T: Well then, what age was he when he learned to read and write Irish, and what was his reason for learning to do so at all?

Ó C: He had a really great love of Irish and there was a certain amount of teaching through Irish on the Blasket before Tomás' time. Irish was being taught in the Protestant school there and Tomás got to know about it. He also knew those people who could read and write Irish. There was a wonderful man in Dunquin by the name of Seán Ó Muircheartaigh whose mother was an Ó Criomhthain woman and Tomás was a very close relative of hers. Whenever Tomás was held up on the mainland by the weather he used to stay in Seán's house. Neil Chriomhthain's family used to do quite a lot of reading and writing.

T: But he was quite on in years by the time he learned how to do so?

Ó C: He was well on. I think he was over sixty years when he began to read and write Irish because we were being taught Irish in the school on the Blaskets at that time and I had learned how to write letters and words in Irish.

T: Was his spelling accurate?

Ó C: He spelled according to the sound. Indeed it was easy to understand what he wrote because he brought out the full sound of every word, and so his spelling was very long.

T: Who prompted him to take up his pen first day?

Ó C: I'm not sure now who prompted him unless it was Fionán Mac Coluim* who started him off and then Cormac Ó Cadhlaigh. When Cormac went to the Island the Gaelic League sent a dancing-teacher, Tadhg Ó Ceallaigh, in with him. They used to gather for dancing in the national school. Tomás himself was an able dancer, so he was, and a great man for music and songs too. But he started off, I imagine, by writing first for *An Claidheamh Solais* and *An Lóchrann*.

T: Short little articles at first?

Ó C: Short articles and short stories. There's no trace of them now but they could still be found if somebody searched for them, so they could.

T: You were the only person then living with him in the

house on the Island. Seán, could you paint for me a picture of Tomás when he was writing?

Ó C: I could, in a kind of way. I could tell you a little about him but it would not by any means be a full picture. In those days the people on the Blaskets used to have their tea in the evening. They didn't call it an evening meal but evening tea. That was between seven and eight o'clock, and we used to go out after it. There was a table here in the corner at the right-hand side of the fire-place. Tomás would pull up the table. There was a lamp high up on the wall with a mirror on it behind the globe and two wicks, each of them as big as a light-house. Tomás would draw up to the fire. His pipe was always on the hob along with his tobacco. He'd smoke a fine blast of the pipe and then turn around, get his foolscap ready and set to work with his pen, a beautiful one which he had got from one of the visitors. I can't say if it was Brian Ó Ceallaigh or Cormac Ó Cadhlaigh who gave it to him, but I still remember the name on it, Waterman's.

T: Is that so?

Ó C: That is so. It was a Waterman's fountain pen, and every night when finished with it he'd dry it with a piece of cloth and a bit of paper and put it away. If a butterfly or a cricket in the corner as much as touched it he'd nearly kill them. Not a hand was to be laid on the pen in case it might be damaged.

T: How long used he spend writing every night?

Ó C: He used to write depending on how long the house was quiet, and according as thoughts occurred to him he'd put the finishing touches to them, and he was often writing when I came home. It might be ten o'clock or half-past ten and Tomás would still be on the pen.

T: Well, *Allagar na hInise* or *Island Cross-talk* was his first book. Could you tell me who encouraged him to write it?

Ó C: I'm the one to answer that. Brian Ó Ceallaigh was the man who prompted him to write every book he wrote. Brian it was who told him to have a shot at it and he started him off like this: 'Tomás,' said Brian, 'write down everything you see tomorrow, no matter what it is. Today is Monday. Write down everything you see on Monday and come again on Tuesday. Continue on and write down what you see on Tuesday. Keep going and write down everything you see every day of the week, and

113

when you have filled a certain number of pages of foolscap put them into an envelope and send them to me in Killarney. I'll keep them safely.' Tomás continued on writing and writing a diary and from that came *An tAllagar* that we have today.

T: I see. By the way who was this Brian Ó Ceallaigh?

Ó C: He was a gentleman. Every stranger who came to the Island was called a gentleman. No matter what kind of a tinker came the islanders called him a gentleman because they knew nothing about nobility or any such thing, so the stranger was always described as a gentleman. Brian didn't have much Irish. In fact he was very weak at it and didn't like talking to the visitors. He knew, however, that Tomás could understand everything he said because Tomás had English. They say that he was a secondary school inspector or something like that.

T: Very good, Seán. Well now, let us leave *An tAllagar* for the moment. It appears that Tomás was very reluctant to write the story of his own life known now as *An tOileánach*.

Ó C: Oh, he was. He was kicking against it, boy. He maintained that he had nothing worth starting with and that he had no idea how to start or finish it. But then, you understand, Ó Ceallaigh knew what he himself was looking for and knew that Tomás could provide it, but Tomás himself didn't realise that he could. So Ó Ceallaigh gave him two books written by some Russian writer. I'm not sure whether his name was Jorkie or Jurkie.

T: Maxim Gorky?

Ó C: That's it. He gave him *My Childhood* and *In the World*. Tomás read them and understood them well. 'I declare to the devil,' he said, 'he's a fellow just like myself.' He then got another book *The Growth of the Soil* from Finland and read it, and the man who wrote that was worse off than the first fellow. He had a tougher life than Tomás himself. When Tomás saw that those poor simple people had come out and described their own lives, 'Yerrah,' said he, 'if they're fools I'll make a fool of myself too. I'll have a shot at it.' He took up his pen and continued writing until finally the well ran dry.

T: Do you have any idea as to how long it took him to write the book?

Ó C: Do you know, to the best of my knowledge from the

time he began *An tAllagar* until he finished *An tOileánach* I'd say he was writing for six or seven years. He also used to write essays for *An Lóchrann* and other such publications. He was all the time writing.

T: I presume that his other books came out later, *Dinnsheanchas na mBlascaodaí* and *Seanchas ón Oileán Tiar*.

Ó C: I think it was Bláithín who collected from him the material in those two books.

T: Do you mean to say that Bláithín wrote that material down?

Ó C: I'd say so. I make out that Bláithín wrote those stories down from Tomás' oral account.

T: Well, I suppose you were going to school when he began writing?

Ó C: Indeed I was.

T: Did he ever ask you to solve any problems for him?

Ó C: He never gave me any problem to solve except maybe a word which he wasn't too sure how to spell. 'Look at this,' he might say to me. 'See if this is correct. Is that how ye spell it in school?' I'd reply: 'You're better at it than we are at school. Carry on.'

Did you ever see any example of his handwriting?

T: No, I didn't. What was his handwriting like, by the way?

Ó C: Oh, it was wonderful altogether. It really was.

T: He composed poetry also, didn't he?

Ó C: Oh, he used to compose poetry all right. He composed quite a lot of poetry. Didn't he write a long poem about the people of Uíbh Ráthach or South Kerry? It's available but I haven't got it.

T: I see. When used he compose the poetry?

Ó C: He used to compose it while working. When he was cutting turf and got tired – in those days the tea sold by Kruger's mother and Pats Neidí's wife in Dunquin, may the Lord have mercy on them, was packed in white paper pound bags. Tomás always held on to those white bags. They were very handy for him because he'd put them into his pocket together with a pencil, and he composed most of his poetry when going to the strand or up the hill saving turf. He'd sit down on a little mound, have a smoke and write down the verses. He'd come home then in the evening, take out one of those big donkeys of foolscap pages, write down the verses and then send every piece he had composed to Fionán.

T: To Fionán Mac Coluim?

Ó C: To Fionán Mac Coluim. Tomás knew Fionán well long before he got to know *An Seabhac.**

T: I see. Well did he ever think that the day would come when his work would become famous not only in Irish but in other languages also?

Ó C: He hadn't the slightest idea that he would ever see a book of his in print because not much was being published in Irish in Tomás' time.

T: Did he continue to write until the end of his days?

Ó C: He continued to write until his hand and leg became paralysed.

T: Is that what caused him to stop writing?

Ó C: That is what stopped him. He couldn't even raise his hand above his head, so he couldn't, and I recall a matter that he needed to attend to towards the end – it was a document that concerned just him and me. He had to sign it with his left hand.

T: By the way, when did he die? In 1937?

Ó C: He died on the seventh of March 1937, and his remains were brought out to his ancestral graveyard, the old one in Dunquin.

T: If Tomás was alive today do you think he'd be pleased with the fruits of his work and with the state of the Irish language in general?

Ó C: I imagine that if Tomás was alive today there would be no man in Ireland as pleased as himself because of the success of the language movement as well as other things, and the way all those people continue to come back again and again to the West Kerry Gaeltacht with copies of his books, *An tOileánach* and *An tAllagar,* in their pockets. I'd say that he'd feel like the King of Ireland. I was talking to a man in Ballydavid today, a man from the north of Scotland. He had Tomás' book in his pocket and had been talking the day before to Séamas Ó Beaglaoi, the publican, who himself is a great man for Irish. This guy said to me: 'Whisper,' he said, 'are you a son of Tomás Ó Criomhthain's?'

'I am,' I said. 'That's what they call me anyhow but I don't know whether I am or not.'

He pulled the book from his pocket and told me that he was after going west to Dunquin specially to see the Island where the author of *An tOileánach* was born.

'Good man,' said I. 'You did well to go there.'

'Oh,' he said, 'I prefer that book to all the books in the world. It reminds me,' he said, 'of all the islands of Scotland and of the tough life there. I suppose,' he said, 'Tomás had a hard life.'

'I don't think that he had a hard life at all,' I said. 'And if he had a hard life he was by no means poor. His life was free from hunger.'

T: What was his main livelihood, fishing or the land?

Ó C: Fishing, oh the fishing, but the two of them fitted in nicely together. He kept a cow and had his own milk and potatoes, so he had.

T: Speaking of the great number of people who come to the West Kerry Gaeltacht in recent years it can be said that Tomás' work has been largely responsible for that.

Ó C: It is largely responsible as far as I can see, because since I came to live on the mainland I've come across many people and there are only a few of them who haven't read *An tOileánach* and *An tAllagar* as well. They want to trace his footsteps, where he lived, where he is buried, and so on. The same is true of Peig Sayers' work and of *Twenty Years A-Growing*. Those books have some attraction for people.

T: They certainly have. And then there's his most famous remark of all at the end of the book – 'because our likes will never again be seen.'

Ó C: How did he think of that, I wonder? Where did he get that sentence?

T: I don't know.

Ó C: I suppose he had some inkling because the generation that went before him wasn't like himself in any way.

T: As well as that he probably noticed that the Island was failing.

Ó C: He did, and why wouldn't he? As he himself remarked one day when those who were strong and energetic were abandoning the Island and going away: 'What will we do when the clay pipe is broken? They won't be able to launch a boat,' he said, 'or take a boat up out of the water. They won't be able to knock a cow or tie her to put her into a boat.' That was the situation.

T: Seán, when you were young and looking at your father writing every night did you yourself ever get the urge to write a book?

Ó C: No, never, because I didn't know the meaning of the word 'book' at that stage. I used to laugh at Tomás and pull his leg when I'd see the poor wretch bent down over the table and writing every night and I had no understanding of matters that Tomás understood so well.

T: But did you attempt to write anything then, essays or such things?

Ó C: I used to write little articles for *An Lóchrann* and other magazines, *An Scuab* and so on, but I wrote those in school and after leaving school I gave no thought to books or reading or writing, nothing only the outdoor life.

T: You gave up the pen completely?

Ó C: I gave up the pen completely. We went fishing and we went out with the girls and so on, keeping late hours out under the sky.

T: Ye were too busy.

Ó C: We were too busy. But those things came and went and I saw Tomás' work and the sorry state of the Island, with the boys and girls I knew having gathered themselves off out of my sight, and the Island falling away and fading. Even the old people were dying. Men and women in their bloom had gone away and houses were being abandoned. One house last year, another this year and two houses the third year, so that soon twelve were empty. I realised then that something would have to be done about writing all that down for posterity, so I said to myself that I'd write *Lá dár Saol* as I saw it. That is what put the thought into my head so I took up my pen and got my foolscap and wrote away. I continued on writing until told to stop.

T: But you didn't follow the pattern of the other books from the Island.

Ó C: No, I didn't. I had already read them and felt that there

118

was no point in rewriting what they contained. What I had to say hadn't been mentioned or referred to by any other writer. Neither *Twenty Years A-Growing* nor Peig nor Tomás had mentioned it because it hadn't happened to the same extent in their time as it had in mine.

T: How long did *Lá dár Saol* take you to write?

Ó C: Well, I'd say that I completed it within four months because it was just a matter of putting the material down on paper. The story and the account came into my mind as freely as a stream runs downhill. I had no problem.

T: It appeared around the year 1969, didn't it?

Ó C: It did indeed, around the year 1969.

T: Are you pleased with the book?

Ó C: Well, I felt it was cut down too much. The essays and chapters in it should have been slightly longer because after reading it you'd enjoy the additional material all the more, you understand. The chapters are too short. It's a great pity that more conversation wasn't included, if that was possible.

T: But why it was cut down in your opinion?

Ó C: I haven't an idea unless it was the cost of printing or something like that.

T: Are you saying that you were told not to write or include too much?

Ó C: Oh, I'm by no means saying that I was told not to include too much but I'd write more if it was going to be included, you understand. I don't really know what happened but we have to take it as it is.

T: Do many people come to talk to you about the book?

Ó C: They do, they do. They bring it with them and I have to put my signature, the animal's signature as the man said, on the cover, and they have little notebooks containing a lot of words and sentences that they don't understand and they ask me to explain them. But no nuns come.

T: Why is that?

Ó C: I don't know. They say that I was too hard on them.

T: By the way talking of being hard on people, do any nuns call into you who don't agree with things you said in the book?

Ó C: Some of them. Some of them call in, and they love the book. Others come in who don't like it because I said that they

119

hadn't any special qualities and weren't productive. They themselves say that they were very productive.

T: Would you like to undertake the writing of another book?

Ó C: I would if I had the material and was in the way of doing so. But I don't think that there's anything left in my head now unless I started with old tales and I have no interest in them.

T: But I don't think that you are completely drained.

Ó C: I don't know. I'm not drained at all in that way. I feel now that small books containing simple Irish would be very suitable for those students who are learning Irish, short simple little sentences which wouldn't be difficult and would explain the story clearly.

T: Do you think that the Irish in the books we are discussing, your own book for example, *Twenty Years A-Growing*, *The Islandman*, *Peig* and so on is too rich and too difficult for students?

Ó C: I think that it is too difficult for them because the simpler the language the more acceptable it will be to them. I know what learning a language is all about. When we were compelled to learn English, simple English, at school we didn't shirk the job, but when we came across difficult problems which required the use of a dictionary we didn't like them. However if the exercises were short and easy you'd learn a lot of English from them and you'd gradually learn how to handle the problems.

T: Were the boys and girls who were in school with you interested in learning English?

Ó C: They were very interested in English. We were much more interested in English than in Irish because we enjoyed it even though we got many a good wallop from the teacher when we didn't understand it properly, but after leaving school we used to gather together and read not Irish but English. We were thinking of another country and of life beyond the Island. It was then the intention and plan of everyone on the Blaskets to go to America and English was necessary for you to do anything there and to understand the people.

T: Even if you or indeed any of the people on the Island wished to read Irish books at that time I don't suppose such books were available.

Ó C: Well, Tomás used to get little books containing Irish lessons from the Gaelic League. When the League was established Fionán Mac Coluim and others used to send us books and those books were in great demand. Peig Sayers' son Micheál, known as 'The Poet' – he's dead now, may the Lord have mercy on him – and Muiris Ó Suilleabháin *(Twenty Years A-Growing)* would call to Tomás every evening of the week and they were the most wonderful pair I ever saw to study Irish. Tomás would read for them and they learned how to read from him. They made great progress and Tomás was delighted in his heart to have them as pupils. And when *Twenty Years A-Growing* first came to the Blaskets after being in care in Dingle he spoke only English. All he had was English. He went to school on the Island but he soon lost all his English and became very fluent in Irish, so he did.

T: But I presume that the children and parents also were very interested in English since they were destined for the emigrant ship.

Ó C: They were, honestly they were, and the parents loved to hear the youngsters and the children reading English.

T: I suppose that some visitors came to the Island in those days who didn't have any Irish.

Ó C: Many of them had no Irish.

T: How did they manage?

Ó C: They managed as the French fishermen did, with signs. We helped them out.

T: Do you remember any of them in particular?

Ó C: I can remember only one man, a Mexican. He hadn't a word of English or Irish, just his own language. Yet all you had to do was make signs as you would with a dog that you'd be setting after sheep. He was very nice, very polite and had Irish before he finally left, so he had.

T: And how did he happen to come to the Island first day?

Ó C: He came by Dunquin and Dingle and as a result of something he had read in his own country.

T: Did you yourself pay any visit to the Island recently?

Ó C: I wasn't on the Island now, I imagine, for the past ten years. I was in the company of a group who were here doing a course in Science or Rural Science. They went in, and myself and

Micheál Ó Gaoithín, 'The Poet', may the Lord have mercy on him, were with them that day.

T: Did it make you feel lonely?

ÓC: No, not at all. Isn't it strange, I was delighted that there was nobody there.

T: Why?

Ó C: Because of the hardship we suffered there and the peace and the fine life that people living on the mainland enjoyed. Those who visited the Island with us were delighted to be there because the day was fine, you understand. It was a picture of a day, but if they were there in winter-time without any tobacco and a rough sea full of spray coming from the northwest they'd have a different tune. No, it didn't make me lonely. I was delighted that there was nobody still living there because I know only too well what it was like.

***

T: Seán, what were the difficulties which people on the Island experienced when a child was being born?

Ó C: Sometimes there were serious difficulties but it wasn't so bad if the weather was favourable. But if the weather was bad and things weren't going too well for the woman about to give birth, and the midwife told the people that she couldn't bring the child into the world without the aid of a doctor or a nurse who was skilled in that work, then four men had to be got. They'd carry a nayvogue down to the slip, board it and row out against the wind. It made no difference what the wind and sea were like, that is, of course, if the nayvogue could make the journey at all. Then one of them would have to get a horse in Dunquin and bring word to the doctor in Dingle because there was no way of talking to or contacting him, no telephone, no nothing in Dunquin. It might take you four hours to bring the doctor to Dunquin and maybe it might take you another two hours to reach the Island. The woman would still need help, but as soon as the doctor arrived with the proper equipment her problems were over. He'd deliver the child and give the woman whatever treatment she needed. The woman of the house and everyone in the village – all the houses in those days were bang up against one another – were happy as could be, so they were.

T: Incidentally were the doctors sometimes reluctant to go into the Island in bad weather?

Ó C: I don't think they were. I never heard of any priest or doctor who was reluctant to go to the Island, never.

T: Supposing it wasn't necessary to bring a doctor to the woman how did ye manage?

Ó C: Oh, there was a woman on the Island, a sort of a trained nurse who was known as the midwife and she was well able to do what needed to be done. She carried out the whole operation just as well as the doctor would. She looked after the baby and dressed him and knew how to handle the situation properly. But if there was a special problem she wouldn't tackle it, you understand, in case she might kill the baby, perhaps, or smother it or something like that. She'd steer clear of the problem. In that case the doctor would have to be brought in.

T: At what age were the children baptised?

Ó C: Well now, it is like this. If a few women were due to give birth fairly soon after one another the baptism might have to wait until three or four children were born. That meant that the first child born might be two years old. They'd have to bring the children out to Dunquin and get a man and a horse to take them north to Ballyferriter. They'd need to send word to the priest a couple of Sundays beforehand that such and such a number of children from the Island was coming out to be baptised. That meant that he'd be ready for them. They'd have a great day when three or four children were baptised together.

T: Did the father and mother, or rather the fathers and mothers, come out with them?

Ó C: Ah no, just the other women, those who were fit to come out, but the mother of a year-old or a two year-old child would come out all right, so she would. The godmothers and godfathers would also come, and they'd all go to the priest's house. That's how it was done.

T: They'd have a great day in Ballyferriter?

Ó C: Oh, they would, a 'wet' day, particularly the old people. They'd talk about the great event, that so-and-so had a young child who was named after him, and it might be that same man's seventh or eighth or even ninth child.

T: Were there any superstitions connected with baptism?

Ó C: There were. I know of one superstition which I often heard mentioned. In the case of a woman who was going to have a child no red ember was ever allowed to be taken out of the house during her pregnancy until the child was born. Many is the time a man went into a house for an ember from the fire to patch a damaged nayvogue or some such thing. He'd go to one of the houses in the village, and after going in he'd make for the tongs and take it in his hands. But the old woman would raise her hand saying: 'Leave that in there until the things that are inside come out.' He'd go off out for himself then.

T: What were they afraid of?

Ó C: Afraid that the child mightn't be formed or shaped properly or something like that, or that some being that I'm not aware of might have power over him. But look, superstitions did exist. Then there was the stale urine or *maothachán* if you know what that is. Many people know about it nowadays. That would have to be sprinkled every night as soon as the child was born. The stale urine was the first thing to appear, not the holy water but the stale urine. It was sprinkled in the yard and around the house on the outside. It was sprinkled on everybody inside and on everybody who came in. Before anyone left the house they got a dash of it.

T: What was the reason for that?

Ó C: Oh, fear of the fairies and that the child or the child's mother might be blighted. It was a protection against the enemy, the pookas or the fairies as they were called here.

T: Tell me, what games did children of two years, three years, four years play?

Ó C: Children of two years on the Island had no games. You had to wait until you went to school when you were five years old.

T: How were they kept away from the sea?

Ó C: Indeed many is the time they weren't, but the older children had nothing much to do except to mind the smaller ones and take them by the hand. There were glens and cliffs there and children might fall down into the glens or over the cliffs. There was one particular glen that they had to be careful of. It ran east to the pier. There's a path at the edge of that glen near the top of the cliff and no young child was allowed to go there unless another child had a hold of him because if he staggered at all he was gone. But people were very careful in this regard, so they were.

T: You say that children went to school at the age of five.

Ó C: The child was brought to school at the age of five. The oldest children in the house brought him. The oldest girl or boy had to take the young child by the hand, bring him to school and back home again in the afternoon. If there was a child in a house who had nobody to bring him to school some other girl on her way to school would call for him and bring him there and back home again in the afternoon. She might get a few pence or a little present from the woman of the house at the end of the week.

T: Where would the girl spend those few pence?

Ó C: She'd bring them home. There was no place to spend them so she'd hand them over to her mother. If in six months' time or so the girl needed a school-book or something her mother would go to where the girl had put aside her few pence and take them.

T: The school, of course, was within a hundred yards of every house on the Island.

Ó C: It was, a hundred yards and it wasn't even that much from some of them, so it wasn't.

T: Where did the teachers reside?

Ó C: When the school was first founded on the Island the teacher lived in it. Himself and his wife had a room near the gable-end and if he had children they lived there also but the most recent teachers on the Island got a house of their own if they were married and if they weren't they got rooms in some other house. One of the teachers who taught me was married with a wife and family when he came. He got a house on the Island and spent quite a while there. But to go back further the first teacher ever to go to the Island got a small house near the school gable for himself and his wife and children, so he did. He used to cook his own food there as he had a fire and a chimney and all there.

T: I presume that everything was taught through Irish in that school.

Ó C: It was but when I first went to school no Irish was being taught. The teacher was unmarried and a great man for drink and for English but he had no interest in Irish. Then when this other teacher came he started off with little Irish lessons and showed us how to write our names in Irish. His knowledge of spoken Irish was terrible but he was always talking to us and to the girls and boys who were, as you might say, in the senior classes. It was from them that he learned his Irish.

T: But Irish was the language spoken by the teachers?

Ó C: It wasn't. This fellow couldn't use it as his everyday language. He always spoke English except now and then.

T: Even to the islanders?

Ó C: Even to the islanders, and his wife did so as well. He spent only two or three years on the Island. He studied and learned Irish and in the end he was very good at it although you couldn't say he was really fluent.

T: How many teachers were there usually in the school?

Ó C: Ever since I began going to school there were two, so there were. There was the Master who was known as 'The Big Master' and there was a woman who taught the smaller children. She used to teach them sewing and such things, and she taught them lessons as well. But she had fluent Irish, so she had.

T: Did ye get homework to do?

Ó C: We certainly did, towards the end.

T: Towards the end you say?

Ó C: Yes, when we grew up into the senior classes. We certainly did.

T: At what age did the boys and girls leave school?

Ó C: Once you reached a certain age the teacher wouldn't allow you to go to school any longer. He'd throw you out. If you were coming anywhere near sixteen, I think, he'd show you the door. He had no class for you. There was no other class beyond the eighth. If you wanted to continue and if he was thankful to your parents in any way he might allow you to stay on for another six months.

T: By the way the islanders, at least most of them anyhow, had beautiful handwriting. What do you think was the reason for that?

Ó C: I suppose they learned it and picked it up from one another. I can't say if the teacher was responsible. But this lady teacher we had used to come round to us every day, I think, and hold our hands with the pen between our fingers and show us how to form the words. Then we had a book known as the 'headline copy-book,' so we had. That was wonderful and we imitated that a lot. Then again if your handwriting or penmanship wasn't good they made fun of you and there was nothing you hated more than to be made fun of in class. You'd make the effort.

T: How did ye find the learning of English?

Ó C: Terrible, terrible. The first English word I ever heard in school was 'donkey'. The teacher had a picture of a donkey and he wrote the Irish word *asal* on one side of it and donkey or ass on the other. From then on he used to get a picture of a sheep or a rabbit or a goat, and especially pictures of boats and sails, and he'd write down the Irish and the English for them. Then he started us off reading English, a few short sentences from simple books. But do you know something, when we were advancing or growing up, as you might say, we got a liking for it, for English I mean, and in our last years in school we were far keener on learning English than on learning Irish. We knew that we had sufficient Irish so we wanted to have English. We really loved it and every one of us who went to the school on the Island learned enough English, including reading and writing and speaking, to take us anywhere in the world.

T: Did ye try speaking English around the Island itself?

Ó C: No, we didn't. There wasn't a hope of that, so there wasn't. Those who left school had English books and used to read them during the winter, and also when they were herding cows or drawing home turf or going for turf they carried the book with them in their pocket and they used to read it.

T: Where did they get those books?

Ó C: They got them from the visitors who used to come to the Island in those days, and relatives of their own who had gone overseas to America used to send them papers and books and magazines and so on.

T: Do you recall what kinds of books they used to get?

Ó C: Yerrah the most widely read paper I saw was *The Daily Sketch*, a great big paper, and that used to do the rounds from house to house. Some man from England used to send it over. And then when the lobster ships came – large companies used to send big boats to the Island for lobsters – they'd give a lot of papers to the fishermen. Oh yes, and we had an English book in school. I don't remember the name now, *Macbeth* or something like that.

T: Surely ye didn't study *Macbeth* in school?

Ó C: Upon my word we did.

T: And did ye understand it?

Ó C: We did and we loved it. Ours was a small little book. I had *Macbeth* the last two years before I left school. I'll remember it forever. It contained a printing error – a rat than run there – and the master came and stuck a piece of paper over the incorrect word 'run' and wrote on it with his pen the correct word 'ran', do you understand? Yes indeed, we had *Macbeth*.

T: In the form of a play or a story?

Ó C: Oh, it was in the form of a story. And we had another book also called *Ballad, Fact and Fancy*, so we had.

T: Was it the teacher who got those books for ye?

Ó C: It was indeed.

T: Now I suppose there were references in those books to life outside the Island, the life in England perhaps, city life and so on.

Ó C: There were and references even to American life.

T: Did ye find it strange?

Ó C: We didn't. No, nor the devil a bit of it. But I'm telling you we got a pounding from English, boy. And nowadays people are surprised if they get a pounding from picking up their own language. And isn't it a funny thing, all those who attended school on the Blaskets and got a pounding from learning and being taught English said, and still say, that they didn't get half enough pounding so that they'd have a better knowledge of it.

T: Were the teachers in the school very cross? I presume they had a stick.

Ó C: They weren't cross at all. You'd have to be very thick. Maybe we might say when we were growing up that they were cross, but when you'd really understand the job they had to do, they wanted to leave their mark on us, but we didn't realise it. That was the reason for it.

T: You know that children are always trying to avoid the teacher.

Ó C: Indeed they are. I suppose it's their nature.

T: Ye had no hope of avoiding teachers?

Ó C: We could avoid them all right, but there was no point in it because maybe some old man going out to get the donkey would spot you in a hole or beside a fence. He'd come home then and give the game away. And if you stayed away from school any day and your parents found out that you were absent you'd never again go ahide. Every inch of you would be as black as the hob from the hammering you'd get.

T: The people of the Island, particularly the parents, had a great desire for education.

Ó C: They had indeed, and they had even a greater desire for English.

T: What games did children going to school play?

Ó C: The main one that I know of at any rate when I was going to school was jackstones. Three or four of us would play them on the floor in the afternoon after coming home from school and upon my word we often gave one another a good clouting because of them when we'd make a mistake or do something we shouldn't do. The rules were strict. You'd have to play them like you'd play cards. There were five stones. You'd throw one up in the air, catch two that were on the ground, pick them up and catch the one in the air before it fell on the ground, and if it did fall on the ground you threw them away. Then you had three to put together. They were known as the target.

T: The target?

Ó C: Yes, the target. You'd have four altogether in your hand. You'd throw one up in the air and put the other three down on the ground, catch the one in the air, throw it up again and then catch hold of the three on the ground before the other one fell down.

T: What sort were those jackstones?

Ó C: Stones from the strand, Kerry diamonds, if you know them. They are lovely round stones. You'd see them knocking sparks out of one another when they were banged together. On winter nights eight of us used to play partners, that is four a side, and you'd put in as many units as you wished, forty or fifty of them,or if the night was cold or hardy you might put in only ten. We had football too. The ball was known as a sock-ball.

T: How did ye make the sock-ball?

Ó C: From a sock vamp. We used to cut about six or seven inches off the top of the sock. That was done with a shears – there was no such thing as a scissors on the Island then. We sewed the bottom end and filled it with hay or straw or anything else you could get that was dry. That gave it a bit of weight and then you sewed the top end. It was nice and round, so it was. We'd throw the ball into a field and make two halves of whatever number of us was there. There might be six or seven a side and even if there were fifteen a side they'd all be allowed in.

T: How long would the sock-ball last?

Ó C: It usedn't to last long at all especially when it got wet. We used to play in red ground. We weren't allowed to play in any field where there was anything growing for fear the donkey or the cow would have nothing to eat after us. You'd have to go into red ground or west to the strand. The strand was very suitable, so it was, when the tide was out.

T: Did ye have goalposts?

Ó C: Indeed we had. Two stones would be put down as marks and then two other marks a little bit out from them, one on either side. Those were the two point-scoring areas. If the ball went between the two stones on either side you got a point. Points weren't scored over a cross-bar but between the two marks on either side. The cross-bar ye used to have when ye were playing football long ago was up high but our point-scoring area was on the outside, so it was. We used to give one another a real hammering.

T: Of course ye didn't have any football boots?

Ó C: We wore hob-nailed boots. Yes, and if you got a belt of a hob-nailed boot on the shin the mark would be on your shin-bone for two months. It would indeed. We often gave one another a wallop too. However a man came to the Island later on and he had one of those footballs that hop and we used to go playing it. Every one of us would give it a belt of a kick, then a gust of wind would come and blow the ball into the sea. A nayvogue would have to be got then to get the ball back.

When this teacher named Savage came he'd buy potatoes from you if you had them, and when the potatoes were being dug four or five of us would go and steal some. We'd take a bucketful from one man and a bucketful from another and so on. We'd carry a bagful on our backs to Savage and he'd give us money for them. With that money we'd buy a football. That was known as a bladder football. If anyone was going to Dingle we'd send for a football and it would arrive in due course.

T: A real one?

Ó C: Yes, a real one.

T: How much did a football cost in those days?

Ó C: It didn't cost a whole lot then really. Ours was a small one. It wasn't very big at all and the leather was of poor quality. It didn't last long.

T: But was there any level field on the Island where you could play a proper match?

Ó C: There wasn't. Sure we had no place to play this football except on the strand, so we hadn't. The fields were too small and if you had any good kick at all you'd send it into another man's field. Then you'd have to climb over wire. The fellow who went after it might give it two good kicks straight up in the air, and another fellow would say: 'Look at him back there. The devil won't give it back to us at all tonight. He's kicking it up into the air for his own enjoyment.' But the strand was the place for football.

T: Did the girls play football?

Ó C: No then, the girls didn't play any football. I suppose it wasn't worth their while trying.

T: But did they have games of their own?

Ó C: Jackstones, that's what they played. Of course we also had boats, small nayvogues which we made ourselves with a sail and a length of twine on them and a bit of net-cord. We'd release them off out from the strand to see which would go the farthest, you understand. Then we'd haul them in and let them off out again. That's how we spent the evenings after school.

T: What about swimming? Did ye swim at all?

Ó C: We used to swim all right. We'd steal out from school to go for a swim. We'd put up our hands. That was the way you'd get out. You'd put up your hands, you understand, the master would nod his head and you'd dash off out. The pier was as near to us as that river outside. There was nothing to it

131

only gallop down, throw off the duds, jump in and swim two strokes, put on the duds again and run back up. For all the master knew you might have been on your haunches beside the fence, and he couldn't care less.

T: I don't suppose ye had any swimming togs?

Ó C: None. Streakers, stark naked, boy!

T: But ye loved swimming?

Ó C: We did. Every damned one of us could swim, so we could, and the old people were good swimmers too.

T: What age were the children when they went for Confirmation, Seán?

Ó C: I make out that they were nearly thirteen, from thirteen on at any rate, from that to fifteen. And to tell you the God's honest truth when I was going for Confirmation I was after spending a season lobster-fishing with my father, so I was, and the reason was this. The girls would be sent out to the mainland two days before the bishop was due to come and they'd stay in relatives' houses, but the boys wouldn't go out at all. They'd have to be sent out on the morning of the day of the bishop and a car would be got in Dunquin to bring them north to Ballyferriter.

T: A horse and car, of course?

Ó C: A horse and car, yes, or a mule and car. I remember well that some of them had a mule. The day came anyhow and the Master was still on the Island. He didn't go out at all since the boys were to go out the next morning and he'd be with them. But, do you know, this particular morning there was a north-westerly gale from the sea and the waves were crashing in over the reefs. We were still on the Island. So was the Master and he was out of his mind. The bishop was coming but the Master was on the Island and couldn't come out. That put us back three years. That's why we were old, seven of us. We had to wait another three years, you understand.

T: Without being confirmed?

Ó C: Yes, without being confirmed. We were thrown out of school and into the prow of a nayvogue fishing for crabs and eels and lobsters. Then our turn came again and during the third year, when the bishop was due to come, the Master brought us into school every Sunday and gave us lessons. Yerrah every one of us had most of the Catechism off by heart because we were after learning it well at school. Anyhow Confirmation Day came and upon my soul, if it did, the Master didn't wait until the morning this time, boy! He had bought sense and gathered himself off out the evening before. We stayed on the Island. There wasn't a hope that we'd go out, but we struck off out in the morning about seven o'clock, and no better lads to do it as we could row and do our job as well as any old man on the Island. We hauled the boat up on the cliff in Dunquin, headed out through the Gap of Carhoo where you now have your house, down the other side and on east to Teeravane without a car or mule or horse or donkey. We came out of the fields on to the road at Teeravane and away with us east.

T: Did ye always look forward to coming out to the mainland?

Ó C: Ah, we were looking forward to coming out that time. We were drinking like the devil, so we were. Hadn't we the Bandon Rattler on the Island then!

T: Was it on sale there?

Ó C: It was, in a speak-easy. Still it wasn't really a speak-easy because the guards knew well that it was being sold there but they looked upon it as a drink for the benefit of the fishermen. Anyhow the Master was keeping an eye on us because he was well aware of what we were up to and what we might do. He was waiting for us in Ballyferriter just west of the village where the forge is.

'God bless ye!' he said.

'May you live long, Master!'

'That's a good day,' he said.

'It is so,' said some of us, 'but we're parched with the thirst.'

'Oh, parched or not,' he said, 'ye haven't a hope of getting a drink.'

One of us stood up.

'Even if the bishop was to die now over there on the altar,' he said, 'I'll drink two pints of porter before I go east to the chapel.'

'Oh, God be with us forever!' said the Master.

'Master,' I said, 'you may as well be off with yourself now, so you may.'

We went into the pub and each one of us drank two pints. We wiped our mouths and hit the road east. He was waiting for us at the chapel gate. There was no name under the sun that he didn't call us.

'Oh, ye pack of savages!' he said. 'There's no use in being at ye.'

We went in, and do you know something, two of us were put sitting on the end of the stool along with the children who were still at school! There's no use in talking.

T: Well, did ye have to take the pledge then?

Ó C: You got the pledge from the bishop that time.

T: But after being drinking that same morning?

Ó C: Oh, we took the pledge from the bishop. The only pledge the bishop had to give was one that had no effect. After the bishop confirmed us the Master came and brought us all into the pub because, you understand, we used to cut turf for him and bring it down from the hill. He was great with us in a way but if we didn't do as he said he wouldn't be too great at all with us. He brought us in again and gave us tea and bread in Willie Long's pub as well as food for all the people there. Then we left and went into Ó Catháin's house, as the man said, because we knew Ó Catháin of old. We drank our fill there too. We were fine and merry coming home, so we were, and the Master came home with us.

T: That means that ye were, I suppose, sixteen or seventeen years old before ye were confirmed.

Ó C: We were at least, some of us anyhow, and even though we were that old there were fellows older than us who were confirmed that same day. Would you believe it, there were people there for Confirmation whose own children were being confirmed. They were people who were born and reared on the islands who didn't attend on the appointed day because they couldn't get there. Those old people were confirmed in Ballyferriter the day we were there, so they were.

T: Those were people who were living on an island other than the Great Blasket?

Ó C: Yes, people who were living on islands other than the Great Blasket.

T: By that time, I suppose, ye were thinking of marrying or

at least going out with girls.

Ó C: Oh we were. We were fishing by that time and fishing was hard. We were fishing for lobsters and in wintertime for mackerel. Any night that young people felt like it there was dancing and music on the Island. If the night was fine some lad would bring a melodeon with him back a short distance from the houses. There would be a crowd of them there dancing.

T: Outdoors?

Ó C: Oh yes, a little bit to the west above Goods Strand. It was a great place for dancing and music.

T: What was it like, a grassy patch or something?

Ó C: No, just earth. You know that wherever you have donkeys rolling themselves they destroy the top-sod and the grass, and that meant that there was no grass on it. It was a white clayey place just like the floor of a house. There they played music and danced. The boys were getting crabbed, indeed, and the girls getting old. If a girl took a fancy to you she'd come over. She wouldn't be running away from you at all. Then if you took a fancy to her maybe you'd stay with her, but if you didn't fancy her you'd give a jump, leave her there and go talking to another girl.

T: But would the two of them slip away for a part of the night? By the way all this was at night?

Ó C: Oh, at night.

T: In the dark?

Ó C: Oh, there would be a moon. If there wasn't we would not go back there at all because it would be too dark, you understand.

T: Well, would any boys and girls be noticed slipping away together?

Ó C: I didn't notice that as far as I remember because, you see, there were brothers and sisters around and that sort of thing wasn't allowed. I never saw that on the Island until the visitors came.

T: Does that mean that there was no courting on the Island?

Ó C: The devil a bit, and if there was it was by day, so it was.

T: And where could a couple go?

Ó C: They might hop in over a fence or up the hill a bit, maybe. They'd go some place where people didn't usually go, unless some fellow who might be strolling around on his own, you understand.

T: But the Island was so small that it would have been difficult to get such a spot, I suppose.

Ó C: Not at all. It was easy to find a place there if you wanted to. When the real experts came they brought the girls up the hill. Upon my soul the islandman also knew where to bring them if he felt like it. But do you know something, the situation on the Island when we were young was that they'd be joking and laughing at you if you were going with a girl. They'd say that you were a fool to be on the look-out or watching out for her because in a week or a month's time she might have gone off to Dingle to work as a servant-girl or down to Cork or over to America.

T: So your efforts were all in vain then?

Ó C: Oh, all in vain. She was gone away from you. And as well as that the boys hadn't much interest in the girls because they knew they'd leave. They wouldn't stay on the Island for gold or silver although a few did.

T: Well, how then did the boys find girls to marry them?

Ó C: The boys who married on the Island before me and in my father's time, say, got wives through their fathers. As a fellow on the Island said when he was an old man – he was nearly ninety-two years of age when he died: 'I got a wife,' he said, 'and I got her from my father just like he'd bring a donkey into the house. The exact same way! I had nothing to do with her up to then,' he said, 'and unless I married her my father would put me out of the house and give the girl to my younger brother.' That's how many of the boys got married.

T: And so the younger brother would get both the girl and the place?

Ó C: He would, and he did. That happened. And another thing about it, when the eldest son married and had spent a year in his parents' house and had a child born to him, maybe, the father and the second son would go and build a house for him. They'd give him a plot or two of land, put him out and let him make a living, himself and his wife. Then the second son would be looking for a 'donkey' for himself. He'd bring another girl into the house, so he would.

T: Well, I suppose that most of the islanders were very closely related after a while?

Ó C: Oh, they were, they were. They were all the one in the end.

T: What did they do then to get a wife? Go out to the mainland for her?

Ó C: Yes, out to the mainland. There were many superstitions connected with that. That was the reason why matches were made. Matchmaking made sound sense and was very successful. Three or four from either side were needed to make a match, as you know better than I do probably.

T: Supposing a man had a choice what sort of a wife would he like to get? Or what sort of a wife would a father want for his son?

Ó C: Well, her history would have to be looked into to see on what side the blemish was, if there was any blemish. If you yourself weren't aware of it maybe Diarmaid or Donnchadh or someone might know about it. Questions would be asked. If they came here to the Parish O'Moore, say, looking for a wife, they'd send their friends or relatives here to investigate and make enquiries to find out if there was any blemish on her. They did not care what the blemish was as long as there was no slate missing. They considered that to be the worst of all.

T: And all this was done unknown to the young man?

Ó C: It was, and unknown to the girl too.

T: Supposing a match was made when would the couple meet?

Ó C: Indeed I think that matches were made mostly on fair days or market days in Dingle.

T: Yes, but when would the boy and girl meet for the first time?

Ó C: God knows I think that a boy from the Island would not meet the girl who was going to tie the knot with him, if she was from the mainland, until he saw her at the chapel in Ballyferriter.

T: On the morning of the wedding?

Ó C: On the morning of the wedding. She could be covered in warts for all he knew until then.

T: What about the dowry?

Ó C: Oh no dowry was expected with a girl marrying into the Island, so there wasn't. A dowry was never looked for. I don't think I ever heard of a girl from Dunquin or from the mainland bringing a dowry into the Island, but girls from the Island brought dowries to the mainland.

T: Why was that? Was it because girls were slow to marry in there or that you were lucky to get even a wife?

Ó C: Ah that was it. That's all you wanted. You didn't want any money with her. There was a good enough living to be made there.

T: Was there a good living to be made on the Island when you were growing up?

Ó C: There was a good living on the Island at the beginning of this century and before it when the fishing for mackerel with nayvogues began. The big boats never fished for mackerel, only the nayvogues. Large ships used to come from the Isle of Man and from Arklow. They used to anchor south in Ventry Harbour and were fitted out to cut up and salt all this liver on board. There was a good price for fish then and even small money was good money. If mackerel were only five shillings a hundred in those days that was good money. Your bag of flour at that time cost from nine shillings and sixpence to ten shillings and meal was the same.

T: When girls from the mainland married into the Island did they settle in quickly?

Ó C: Indeed they did, because they were screaming to move in. Wasn't that where the gold was? There was nothing on the mainland then – a little bit of land and no money to be made out of butter or anything. But there was fish and gold and lobsters inside on the Island. And even those ships which used to come from England buying the lobsters, when they bought them they paid the fishermen in gold. It wasn't silver or bits of paper but gold.

T: You mean sovereigns?

Ó C: Sovereigns and half-sovereigns and even guineas. Yerrah, some of the islanders had a donkey-load of gold at one stage, so they had.

T: Do you think they kept some of it?

Ó C: They did. They kept some of it.

T: That would be worth a fortune nowadays.

Ó C: I don't know if some of them kept it because they were cute or because they were foolish or didn't want to part with it, but they kept it in the end. I think some of them got about one pound fifteen a sovereign for it.

T: One pound fifteen, that is one pound and fifteen shillings?

Ó C: Yes, one pound and fifteen shillings.

T: For a sovereign?

Ó C: A sovereign at that time, yes. And they say that there was a man on the Island and when he changed the sovereigns into notes he had enough money to buy a piece of land for his daughter somewhere around here in Murreagh and that he still had money left over.

T: When a couple married and were expecting their first child was the doctor brought to the woman?

Ó C: I saw that on one occasion. It so happened that I saw with my own two eyes the doctor coming to a woman because the midwife said he was needed. The doctor had to be got and brought to the house as fast as possible. In such cases four men would go out, strong men like yourself. One of them would go to Dingle and the doctor would come back with him as far as Dunquin. Then they'd row in fast to the Island. If the child was born to the woman in her childbed before the doctor arrived and all was going well the usual signal was to send up smoke in a certain place so that the oarsmen wouldn't have to kill themselves or even hurry, but could take it easy and enjoy a smoke. When the doctor arrived everything would be all right.

T: This smoke you mention, was it from a fire that was lit above the houses?

Ó C: It wasn't, but some straw, say, would be brought out or a sheaf of oats or hay or maybe old sacks. You'd throw a drop of oil on them and then set fire to them with a match. That was the signal, just the same as if the telephone rang. That was the signal. 'Everything's all right. There's smoke inside.' In times of need people on the islands to the west of the Great Island used the same kind of signal. If anything went wrong the men back there had no boat of their own available to them because it was a boat from the main island that used to serve them.

T: Back where, Innisvickillane?

Ó C: Innisvickillane. They used the same smoke signal. Whenever you saw smoke something was wrong. The islanders would go back there then. But in the case of this woman in the bed it was a signal, you understand, to take it easy, not to kill yourself, that all was well.

***

T: Talking about America, Seán, was the eldest girl in the family usually the first to go there?

Ó C: The eldest girl always went first because she'd have spent a year or two working in Dingle or somewhere in the countryside near it or some place where she could earn a few pence. She was always anxious to go. She'd also get help from her parents at home and the fare wasn't a whole lot at that time. I think you could get from Cobh to New York for six pounds. When she went to America and thought of her brothers getting in one another's way at home with nothing to do and nowhere to earn a penny only sit in the corner, she'd send the fare over to them one by one as soon as she had earned it. And when the first fellow went over and was earning he'd return the money he was after getting from Máire or Cáit or whoever, and she'd then send that home to yet another member of the family. That's how the youth and vigour of the islanders were destroyed. They went to America.

T: Well suppose, let us say, there were seven or eight in the family how many of them do you think might be left at home in the end?

Ó C: I'll tell you now, then. No one was left, and I saw that happen with my own two eyes. A fireplace where a family of eleven were reared ended up without anyone except the father and mother. The father died as the last son was about to go. The mother was moved out to her relatives' house in Dunquin and her island home was closed down.

T: Wasn't that extremely hard on the parents?

Ó C: It was in a way, but do you know something, the hardship of the world had left its mark on the parents and they understood it, you understand, because they had got word from America telling them how a person could earn a living and make money there without any difficulty whatsoever, getting up in the morning and going to bed at night, not having to bother about a nayvogue or about life's troubles, but just put down the day. That's how it was. And that happened to many others on the Island, so it did. I remember seeing another family in the same situation. All the children went away and finally the parents were moved out onto the mainland where some sort of a hut was built for them.

T: They must have been very lonely after all the family.

Ó C: They were, and so was the whole village, would you believe, to see a fine man emigrate. Yerrah, they'd make you very sad and bring a tear from your eye too, because you knew that you'd never again see them.

T: I see.

Ó C: You knew it.

T: I suppose, however, they had enough means to raise the family on the Island.

Ó C: Oh, they had, and in the end the children reared themselves. The parents on the Island made a lot of money from rearing families because if a house had three sons fishing and earning money during the two lobster and mackerel seasons they gave the money to their parents except for the odd pound or two they kept for sport.

T: Yes, I was just about to ask you what arrangements parents and their family who were earning had with regard to money.

Ó C: Oh when the children were leaving, I mean those who went to America, if their parents had money belonging to them they gave them whatever amount they wished to take with them, but usually the family didn't take it with them.

T: No, what I meant was this. When the young lads were working, for example fishing and earning money, did they give their parents a certain amount every week?

Ó C: They did. Indeed they did, my lad, and they were delighted to have it to give to them because it was the parents who gave them the money to get whatever they wanted, boots and clothes and things like that, and if they ever went shopping the mother was the one who had the purse. It is said that a father's purse isn't lucky but a mother's is. Still and all I suppose that was another one of their superstitions.

T: By the way who kept the money, the father or the mother?

Ó C: There you have it now. Amn't I telling you that the mother was the one who kept the money because it was said that the father's purse was never lucky as he was too mean or too tight to give it to his wife. She was the one who had the handling of the money and her purse was the luckiest. And in a way I could prove that that was the case unless of course she was a bit of a squanderer.

T: So the children gradually grew up and emigrated, maybe, while the parents were growing old and in the end death was drawing near.

Ó C: Death was drawing near, and no wonder.

T: Did they live long?

Ó C: The old men and the old women I saw dying on the Island were over eighty or at least eighty, as you might say. They were indeed, that is unless something sudden happened.

T: Many of them, I suppose, were never inside the door of an hospital.

Ó C: Never. Wasn't my father one of them? He was never inside the door of an hospital. My uncle was another who was never in hospital. But it sometimes happened that they might injure their hands or limbs somehow. When going after sheep they often fell and put out their shoulder, and in that case the doctor might send them into hospital for a fortnight or three weeks.

T: But that had to do with bones.

Ó C: With bones. It had nothing to do with disease, so it hadn't.

T: What was the commonest disease that afflicted them?

Ó C: The diseases that I heard caused most deaths among the islanders were whooping-cough and measles. There was no cure for those two diseases.

T: I suppose that when people were getting on in years and were no longer able to do much for themselves they got great help from the islanders.

Ó C: They did. They got all the help in the world. If they weren't able to go fishing or go up the hill the turf was brought home for them. Everything they needed from the mainland, paraffin and the like, was brought in for them. If a man from the Island was going out to the mainland for goods that were required for the hearth and even if he had enough to do for himself it could well happen that some old man might call one of his children and say: 'Here, take that gallon with you. Give it to your father and tell him to bring me home a gallon of paraffin.' That man might wind up having to bring back three gallons of paraffin as well as his own. No one was refused anything because that was the way it had to be on the Island. It was as if it had a government of its own. If you committed any crime or did anything wrong not one of them would be pleased. You had to follow the straight road always, and if you didn't the islanders would confront you and correct you.

T: When old people became ill and had to be looked after were they sent to hospital or kept at home and have the doctor sent for?

Ó C: Well, some of them were sent to hospital depending on what was wrong with them. If there was anything that needed clearing up that person was usually sent into hospital, but the old people were kept at home and an old woman from the village, a relative, would come in and wash the old man and put clean clothes on him once a week. She'd do his washing and leave the newly washed clothes on him for a week. But every old man was kept clean, so he was.

T: When the day came that a person died what was the situation? What happened?

Ó C: When a person died the bed was searched to see what was under his head! As the man said, 'It's either under his head or under his legs.' That's how it was.

T: You mean the money?

Ó C: The money. Every bed on the Island had a feather mattress because the feathers could be got from the sea-birds. You might find an old sock there with white coins and brown coins and red coins, as they used to call the sovereigns, and notes stuffed into it. You were allowed to keep that. Then you'd have to get a nayvogue and four men, row out to Dunquin, get a horse there, drive to Dingle, get a suitable coffin and all the fare for the wake, as far as the size of the sock would allow! All those things were brought into the Island and the corpse was waked that night. Porter was on sale there so a barrelful of it was provided and everyone got a drink. Because the dead person was old they'd have a night until morning out of him. If he had any relatives in America, you understand, as soon as they heard he was dead and who had come to his aid and who had taken care of everything, it would come in bundles.

T: You mean money?

Ó C: Money. Oh it would, from his family, so it would.

T: I don't suppose any work was done that day or for a couple of days afterwards.

Ó C: No work was done while they were in Dingle getting everything needed for the wake nor on the following day, the day of the funeral. Very often the weather wasn't the best to bring the corpse out. There was nobody then left for the old men but the old women. The old bones related to them, I mean their forebears, were buried in Ventry or Dunquin or north in Dunurlin, and the corpse would have to be brought there.

T: Of course they were keened, I suppose.

Ó C: I never heard an old person being keened on the Island.

T: Even when it was being done outside on the mainland?

Ó C: I don't know. I find it hard to believe. I never heard any old person over eighty being keened. In fact I never remember anybody being keened except the father of a family or the mother of the family, someone who was a big loss, you understand. She'd be keened all right but not a grey-haired miserable little fellow whose life was over.

T: I see. The people would stay up all night?

Ó C: They would and you wouldn't leave the wake-house unless there was somebody with you, nor would you go in there unless there was somebody with you.

T: Was that a superstition also?

Ó C: A superstition, what else? The place was swimming in superstitions.

T: Did ye play wake-games?

Ó C: No, never.

T: You know that they were played in other places?

Ó C: I wonder were they. I never read about anywhere else or about wakes anywhere else. I find it hard to believe that they would play those games.

T: I presume the Rosary was said.

Ó C: It was indeed. I saw that myself.

T: Who used to give it out?

Ó C: The old woman or the old man. An old woman always started it but after that everyone would try to say a decade. There were small sods of turf in every house and if the old woman had her back to you some lad would get three or four of those little sods and hand them around. When this old woman would have finished her decade someone would throw a sod at the wall and she'd look up. While looking up she might get a belt of another sod in her ear-hole. She'd have a drop of whiskey taken, you understand, and she'd jump to her feet.

T: Well how long was the corpse kept in the house, one night or two?

Ó C: Two nights. Supposing he died tonight about four or five o'clock he'd be kept in the house that night and also the night the coffin would come and he'd be removed after that.

T: That's two nights altogether?

Ó C: Yes, he'd stay two nights in the house, so he would. That's the way it had to be.

T: And when would the funeral leave the Island?

Ó C: Do you know something, the funeral would leave the Island according to the tide. The box had to be put into a nayvogue and that was very difficult if the tide was out. You'd have to push the nayvogue out with only two on board and the other man would have to try to board it out in the water, you understand, but they could all go straight from the slip if the tide was in.

T: Was the coffin placed in any special position in the nayvogue?

Ó C: Oh it had to be, so it had. The coffin or box fitted exactly down into the stern of the nayvogue, you know. If you saw it now you'd take no notice of it. The whole box fits down into the stern, even the lid on top. When it is placed down there it is as steady as could be.

T: Would the nayvogue belonging to the house, that is the dead person's house, come out to the mainland also? Or is that the one that would carry the corpse?

Ó C: Oh that was the one. If there was a son of his there he'd have the corpse in his own nayvogue. The relatives would also travel in it, and it would go on ahead with the other nayvogues following behind.

T: Were the nayvogues in any special formation?

Ó C: They were. Any nayvogue carrying only the crew, you understand, wouldn't like to go ahead of the corpse, just as happens on that road outside, so that the corpse was always in front. It was always in front with only three or four men rowing. The nayvogue behind you would never pass you out, so it wouldn't. If the wind was favourable every nayvogue hoisted a sail. The nayvogue containing the corpse would be in front because when conditions are suitable for sailing, you understand, you'll let the wind out of your own sail and allow the nayvogue carrying the corpse to lead the way. You will indeed.

T: Were any prayers said while the corpse was being brought out to Dunquin?

Ó C: No. No prayers were said except those that had already been said on the Island. After that you sprinkled holy water on the corpse, covered the box, closed it tight and carried it away. No matter where you were you wouldn't go to the pier on your way out without going the Boreen of the Dead. If the pier was out there where your car is you'd have to go out this way and up along here and then along the Boreen of the Dead. That was another superstition, if indeed they are superstitions.

T: And when ye reached Dunquin were there people there waiting for ye?

Ó C: Indeed there were. The people of Dunquin were great. They were surely.

T: It must have been extremely difficult to carry the box up to the Top of the Cliff.

Ó C: You had to have six or seven men around it because it would be all the time slipping backwards, so it would. It's very difficult to bring a box up from the Great Cliff.

T: Did ye say any prayers when the corpse was brought to the slip in Dunquin?

Ó C: No prayer at all. I never heard a prayer being said there. Of course the people of Dunquin would take their caps off and say a prayer.

T: What about the road east to Dunquin, to the graveyard?

Ó C: You'd have to go up to Pats Kennedy's house and east along. And the Crossroad of the Dead is east there where you turn downhill. You had to lay the coffin on the ground there and lift it up again and continue on.

T: Without saying any prayer?

Ó C: Oh a prayer would be said at the Crossroad of the Dead. That's why there is such a place as the Crossroad of the Dead, to say a prayer there.

T: Well then, when the old person was buried were there any superstitions, for example, that had to do with his clothes or anything like that?

Ó C: There were, and plenty of them. If the dead man had good clothes everybody's mouth would be wide open hoping to get them. They'd rather have his clothes than have himself alive, so they would. But if you yourself had good clothes you would not be interested in them because they could cause trouble. You'd have to throw off your own clothes and pull up on your own bones every bit of the dead man's clothes, his shirt and drawers and trousers and socks and shoes and cap or hat. And they'd have great fun putting the hat on a fellow who never wore a hat.

T: Suppose the clothes were too big or too small for you?

Ó C: Even if they were you still had to take them, so you had, because there was another thing too, you understand. You'd have to bring them to Mass three times. That was the way. And as soon as the third Mass was over you could, if you wanted to, cut them with the knife and make them fit you. They say that there was this man, anyhow, who got the clothes and hat of a fellow who had died but if they were to cut the head off him he wouldn't wear the hat. He went to Mass and brought all the clothes with him except the hat. What did he do but wear a new cap of his own with the dead man's clothes. But the story is told of a trickster who was after coming home from America and hearing about your man. He was a bit of a wilder in America. Didn't he spread the rumour that he saw Pad with no hat on! The people got to hear about it and there was no talk about anything except that Pad was up at the top of the Boreen of the Dead without a hat on. Your man came down home, slapped the hat

147

on his own head and went to Mass. He took the hat to Mass three Sundays in a row, so he did.

T: What was the idea of bringing the clothes to Mass three Sundays in a row?

Ó C: That was the rule and the custom that had to do with the dead in those days. Isn't it gone out of the world altogether now, isn't it?

T: It is.

Ó C: It is, my lad. I suppose some superstitions came down from olden times. It was some kind of old folklore. It was indeed.

T: Did anyone ever die on the hill or some place like that outside the house?

Ó C: As far as I can remember I never heard of anyone dying like that, but they used to fish for wrasse long ago and a man was lost while fishing.

T: If so it wasn't as a result of illness?

Ó C: No. It wasn't that he died naturally. I never heard that anyone died suddenly on the Island.

T: It is also said that nobody ever died on the Island without a doctor or priest. Is that true?

Ó C: I wouldn't agree at all as far as the doctor is concerned.

T: But didn't someone die without a priest?

Ó C: No one died without a priest in my time there. No, but there's a story told about one of them, an old man. He was over eighty years of age. I saw him myself and knew him well in fact. He had a small little house and damned the one living with him only himself, but he had relatives around the Island and they went out to get the priest for him. The priest was in Dunquin but they wouldn't bring him in because the day was too bad and they were afraid that they mightn't be able to bring him back out again so they came in without him. There was a gale again on the following day and he was lying there waiting to die for two days and was barely alive. But didn't this particular morning turn out fine so they went and brought the priest in. As soon as he was anointed he died, so he did, may the Lord have mercy on him.

T: Well there were midwives to attend to girls who were expecting and so on. Was there anybody with any knowledge of healing or medicine who could come to the aid of an old person or anybody else who might be dying?.

Ó C: There wasn't. I never heard that there was. I never heard that of any such person but there were people who made up potions. There was one man anyhow who never shaved himself and was known as the 'Doctor'. He used to make some sort of potions for people suffering from certain diseases but I don't know how he made them.

T: And did they work?

Ó C: Not at all. They didn't work. You'd imagine they did but they didn't.

Padraig Tyers talking with Nóra Ní Shéaghdha

T: Nóra, when did you first go to the Island to teach?

S: I went to the Island to teach in the autumn of the year 1927 just after I finished my teacher-training in the college in Limerick.

T: Do you remember the first day you went there?

S: Oh yes, I remember the first day I set foot on land there. I've described that in my book *Thar Bealach Isteach* . My first thought was: 'Hasn't Ireland turned out to be a confined place for me?' Nevertheless I accepted life on the Island as I should. I accepted the job and made my own of the people. Indeed they too made their own of me.

T: I suppose they were down at the top of the pier waiting for your arrival.

S: They were. That was the custom on the Blasket and later on I too used to be among the crowd there. There was a group of children, women and men eyeing the new teacher, I suppose, because teachers used to come and go from the Island very often, and I imagine that that wasn't to the children's benefit. However I reached my lodgings and was made comfortable there. When I arrived at the schoolhouse next morning, with my fine big key which I had got from Fr. Browne in Ballyferriter on my way west, all the children were gathered there before me. They were putting their eyes through me. 'God and Mary to ye, children,' I said. 'How are ye?' I heard a little voice here and there saying 'Good'. I opened the door and we all entered. They knew where to sit. Everything was new and strange to me, but there was this kind woman who was a great help to me. She was Bean Uí Dhuinn-shléibhe, the assistant mistress in the school at the time.

T: How many scholars were there?

S: At that time there were forty-two on the roll and the attendance was always good because there was nothing to keep them at home. Even if a gale of wind was blowing they'd still have to come to school. There was no place to hang coats, no crooks, no rooms, and they'd run in drenched wet from the rain with the water running down their faces. That didn't worry them however. They'd shake it off like ducks because they were accustomed to having the salt water blowing into their faces every day of the week and every day of the year.

T: As far as I can recall there was just one room in the school.

S: Just one, and the principal's place was directly inside the door where there was a fairly large table. Bean Uí Dhuinnshléibhe said to me: 'That's your place. I'll be down here.' The fireplace was at the other gable. The benches were big long ones, about seven or eight of them in all, as far as I remember now. Bean Uí Dhuinnshléibhe had the Infants and First and Second Classes and I had all the others up to Seventh Class. My group was facing towards the door while Bean Uí Dhuinnshléibhe's was facing down towards the fire, and any inspector who might come could easily see where the division was because the groups sat back to back.

T: What were they like as scholars, Nóra?

S: They were nice and pleasant and obedient really. Well, because teachers were coming and going so often I suppose they were rather slow at first and not surprisingly they were shy also. Children born on the island weren't accustomed to people but I never had any trouble with them. The teachers and pupils in the school got on exceptionally well together, I must say.

T: I presume English was of special importance to the pupils.

S: It was. They were very keen on English. Who could blame them? If they only went down to Dingle they'd need it, and at that time there was nothing in their heads but America. There was nothing for them at home and so they did their best to learn English which they did as well as they could, I suppose. Of course we taught English through Irish, explaining everything through Irish and learning the verses in English. They were extremely interested in English poetry just as they were in Irish poetry. They had poetry in their blood, I suppose, and they found it easy to learn. They always prepared it well for the following day, as they did their spellings and other things. I certainly hadn't much trouble with them.

T: I don't suppose there was much equipment in the school.

S: There was none at all. Every afternoon after school I had to sit down and draw maps for whatever lesson I intended teaching the following day, or grammar cards or whatever else was needed. Of course it did me no harm. We had been trained for it. I had to do it all and so had the other mistress, and in those days it was at our own expense. Not a penny was to be had from any government towards it.

T: Did you fit in quickly with the grown-ups on the Island?

S: Well I suppose I was shy and distant at first. I was young and light-hearted and perhaps if I had my own way I wouldn't have gone there at all, but I did as I was told by my mother and by our parish priest at the time, Fr Browne, so I accepted the post. However, looking back on it now I'm increasingly glad that I did so because unknown to myself I learned a lot about my own native district while on the Island, and that was something which I hadn't done previously. If I had gone teaching in a strange place outside of my own district I wouldn't have gained all that knowledge.

T: Of course it was a very big change for you, having just left the college, to move into the Island. What did you do each afternoon, and what kind of life did you have there after school?

S: Life? I suppose you would describe it as a lonely life at the beginning, particularly the first winter. I went there in the autumn and of course winter sets in early around here. At first I used to return home every weekend, every Friday afternoon, travelling out by nayvogue with the postman, Seán an Rí, the blessing of God on his soul. He was indeed a helpful man and many is the time he brought me in and out. I used to return home on the Friday and when I'd go back to Dunquin on the following Sunday there might be a storm which would hold me up. There was nothing to do then but stay in Dunquin until there was a lull in the storm, or a *lon* as the Islanders called it in Irish. Perhaps a boat might come out in mid-week and take me into the Island.

So far so good. I was getting away with that for a while from the Department of Education up in Dublin because, as you know, at the end of each month a teacher is required to fill a form showing absences and so on. Those forms were all in English at that time. And the reason I gave for my absences – 'Weather-bound on the mainland'. However that was happening too often for their liking up in Dublin and they wrote to the parish priest. This particular Sunday when I was attending

Mass in Dunquin the parish priest called me over and said 'Norry,' he said – he always called me Norry, 'Norry in the Island' – 'Fill that up', and he handed me a document which I filled up. There were questions as to why I was absent so frequently and so on, and I had no explanation other than to say that I could neither go in nor swim in there because the nay-vogues were unable to come out for me. But people living far away don't understand that. However a reply was sent to the parish priest requesting him to tell the teacher not be absent so often and to remain on the Island. So I had to stay put and that I did. I said to myself: 'I'll do something else now at week-ends. I'll start writing for *The Irish Press* on anything and everything.' And so I began writing short articles, reading books, knitting and so on, and that whiled away the time for me.

T: Is that how you came to write your two books?*

S: Well I wrote those later on. I began with short articles.

T: Incidentally were there any girls of your own age on the Island at the time?

S: There were girls who had finished with school and I made friends with them. They were friendly and very nice indeed to me. I must make special mention of one of them, Lís Ní Shúilleabháin, Seán Ó Criomhthain's wife, who died a few years ago and whose death made me feel very lonely. Lís and I were very close and many is the secret she and I shared with one another. I recall the last day before I left the Island. We were on the While Strand chatting and talking, and Lís was saying: 'Oh indeed I'll miss you.' I would say to her: 'I'll miss you too but still and all I have no business staying on the Island forever. I may as well accept the post which I've been offered now'. I recall the tears falling from my eyes and I'll remember forever Lís' words as she laughed out loud: 'Yerrah Nora,' says she, 'may nothing ever affect your eyes.' I can still see her that day. I hope she's in heaven. There were also other girls, Siobhán Ní Chearnaigh, Máire Ní Ghuithín and Cáit Ní Chatháin and other grown-up girls like them. A crowd of us – a 'bulk' was the islanders' word – would go west below the houses to meet the boys and we'd chat away like any such group would.

T: By the way were there many people on the Island at that time?

S: There were about a hundred and fifty there then, I imagine, including everyone.

T: And was there much poverty there?

S: Poverty? Well I can't say that I witnessed much poverty. Perhaps there was a couple of families who you could say were poor because their children were young. As for the other houses some of the family had gone to America and were sending money home, while those houses from which nobody had yet emigrated and which were dependent on the sea and the fishing had no income except the fish which they caught and the money they got for it. They were certainly poor and could have done with more if they had it, but in each such case the family gradually grew up, went to America and did well afterwards.

T: How many years had you spent on the Island by the time you resigned from the post?

S: Six and a half, and I never noticed the last years passing because I had become like the islanders themselves. I was always a good sailor. I was always very interested in boating. Even when we were at home here in Feothanach we'd go west to the cliff-top at Dooneen in the hope that there might be some young lads there who would take us out boating. We'd be as proud as punch if three or four of us were taken by nayvogue from Dooneen west to Ballydavid and back home again in time for tea. There was no fooling around by night in those times because you had to be a at home before darkness fell.

T: I see. After you left the Island you got a job here in Moorestown, is that right?

S: Yes, here. I got a job here in my native townland and remained here until I retired a couple of years ago.

T: But you hadn't yet forgotten the Island, it seems.

S: I'll never forget the years I spent on the Island. I was just a young light- hearted girl, I suppose, when I went to the Blasket to begin my term as a teacher there, and looking back now I must admit that though I was the teacher the people of the Blasket taught me a lot also because that is where I first heard of and got my first insight into the heroes of our own area. The greatest of them was the poet Piaras Feirtéar.* His poems were on the lips of the old people of the place and they'd introduce some verse of his into every conversation. I remember Seán

Mhicil Ó Súilleabháin. He was full of the poetry of Piaras and of Seán Ó Duinnshléibhe and the other poets and famous people such as Plato. You'd wonder how he got to know about them at all – I didn't know of them – and I was often embarrassed that I knew none of their poetry. Seán Mhicil was a bit of a mocker, always talking about girls and boys and mocking myself and his daughter Lís who used to be with me, joking us about boys and so on. One day he said: 'I know what will happen the boys here, the same as happened Piaras Feirtéar.'

'What's that?' I asked.

'Is it that you don't know the verse?' he asked.

'No, I don't. Say it for me.'

'This,' he said, 'is what Piaras said when his wife didn't remain faithful to him:

The woman I loved best under the sun
For me no love she bore,
Sitting by the shoulder of her lover
And I am left to grieve alone.'

He continued on further but I can't recall any more of it. It's available in Fr Dineen's book about Piaras Feirtéar, of which I have since got a copy. That was the first time I became interested in the poems and life of Piaras. I realised then that there was something lacking in the education I had received in the primary school, and I said to myself: 'Well, whatever I can do for the children of the Blasket regarding local history, the history of their district and of the Island, I'll learn it from the people and then give it back to the children.' That is what I did. I picked out little snippets and little stories from Fr Dineen's book. The children showed a great interest in them because many of them had heard them at home and found them easy to learn, particularly any poem that was close to their own life. I remember that story concerning the seagull. When the English soldiers captured Piaras in Castlemaine one of them spotted a seagull standing on one leg some distance away and he said to Piaras – of course he was only mocking him: 'I'll let you go free if you compose twenty-one verses about that seagull while it's standing on one foot, but only on one condition, that the words 'going west' or 'in the west' or 'to the west' are at the end of each verse.

'I'll try it,' said Piaras, and he started off, but by the time he had composed sixteen verses, I think, the seagull took off up into the air, and the soldiers took Piaras with them to Killarney. But I remember giving the children some of those verses to learn, and you should see how they used to recite from their heart this one about the seagull:

Oh little seagull resting lightly on the lake,
The delightful wave you love the best.
I'm a captive and broken-hearted
While you're so happy to be going west.

There you have the comparison between Piaras the man weighed down by distress and troubles and the little bird without a care in the world and happy as could be travelling westwards on the waves. The children would recite the verse right from the heart. They learned it off and I'm sure that many of them still remember it.

So the people of the Island made it clear to me that my own education was lacking and from that day onwards I made up my mind that in whatever school I might be teaching I'd pass on to the pupils as much local history as I could. And indeed – I may as well admit it now – there were many inspectors who didn't support me in this. I remember one inspector who came to St Eric's School in Moorestown. I had done a story and a little poem with the children concerning St Cuán, and children find it easy to learn a story if it contains a bit of poetry. Indeed it is the easiest way for them to learn a story because they pick it up quickly. This particular child told the story about St Cuán. It is quite a long story about himself and the reptile in Crawley Lake. I can't say if it is true or not but it was part of the tradition and Crawley Lake and Kilquane are real places. The reptile used to come out of the lake and devour the people every seventh year, and one day Cuán went to the lake carrying a large pot. The moment the reptile put its head above water Cuán threw the pot down on top of it and said 'Stay there now until Judgement Day'.

The reptile was below waiting and waiting and finally it spoke:

'It's a long wait till Judgement Day, Cuán,
In cold filthy water,
Only for the pot you placed on my head
I'd devour half and two-thirds of the world.'

Well, the child recited that for the inspector and do you know
the answer the inspector made him? 'I never heard that such a
saint as Cuán existed,' he said, looking sarcastically at me. I was
too shy at that time and scared of inspectors. I didn't give him
any back-chat. I said nothing but put up with his remark.
However I carried on teaching stories that were part of the local
history. Every fine Sunday that came on the Island if I was free
myself and few other girls would sit in the stern of a nayvogue
going out to Mass in Dunquin. The old women hardly ever went
out, just the young men and those men who had the use of their
legs and also the young girls. We loved that because we'd have
a couple of hours outside talking to Kruger Kavanagh or someone else. You'd always meet somebody and the people of Dunquin were certainly very generous to us because they'd never let
you out of the house without your cup of tea or your dinner.
Many is the dinner I ate in Ó Dálaigh's house in Dunquin and
in Máire Sheosaimh's house too, and I shouldn't forget that. The
old women used to say: 'Don't forget eaten bread.' I wish them
all every blessing and if they're dead the blessing of God on
their souls.

On stormy Sundays when I couldn't go to Mass the children
would come to me in the school and together we'd offer the
Rosary to God for all our sakes. I'd have mentioned it to them on
the previous Friday and they'd know well if no nayvogue was
going out to Dunquin. None of them was ever absent because
their mothers would send them along even though they'd also
have the Rosary at home. Their mothers would be on their knees
at home while we were on our knees in the school. I told them
to bring to school any nice prayer which they might have at
home and that I'd be very grateful for it. I remember how on this
particular Sunday Eibhlín Ní Chearnaigh – she's now married
over in Springfield – brought me a piece of paper and said: 'My
mother gave me this for you and said that you might like to
recite it with us.' That prayer was known as the Sunday Prayer

and from that on we recited it every Sunday. See again how I was learning from the island children. The teacher learning from the children! I hope that they too learned something worthwhile from me. In any case here's the Sunday Prayer which I got from Eibhlín:

May we do God's bidding,
May we merit the life of the saints.
May we see the light of heaven.
May the Child Jesus lie with us in bed,
May the merciful Lamb rise with us from our bed,
The Glorious Virgin in our hands to console us,
St Michael as keeper of my soul.
Oh Joyful Mary, oh Glorious Virgin,
Grant that I may see your most revered household,
The Light of Lights and the sight of the Trinity
And the grace to be patient in the face of injustice.

We used to recite that prayer together and I suppose that many of the children had it off by heart afterwards. Religion, by which I mean prayers and Catechism, was the one subject which I found no difficulty in teaching to the Blasket children. How could I! Weren't they hearing it at every hand's turn from morning till night from their fathers and mothers, or their grandfathers or grandmothers if they lived in the house? This interest in the faith was ingrained in them. I suppose that people raised and living on a sea-girt island are so dependent on God, because the sea is all around them as they earn their livelihood, that the faith is part of their very being. The old women used to gather at the well and I remember that on this particular day as the children and I were having a bit of a chat to kill the time, I presume, a stranger came along. He wasn't a Catholic, however. They'd always find out what a person's faith was, but for themselves there was only the Catholic faith. I must say, though, that they never interfered with anyone in those matters and showed no dislike towards anyone who was not of their own faith. In order to get the old women to talk the stranger began to discuss the next world and God, and that didn't go down too well with some of them. Peig Sayers was there anyhow and I suppose she wanted to display her own knowledge. He was saying that there was no such thing as the next world and so on. Some of us were laughing because we realised that he was only joking, but Peig started and said:

> Of course, my friend, neither the wind nor the sun has disap-
> peared,
> Of course, my friend, neither the boat nor the hill has disappeared,
> Of course, my friend the brine hasn't left the fish,
> And of course, my friend, God will forever be merciful.

As you notice there again there's mention of the sea and fish in the middle of the prayer. Gobnait, another woman who was full of lore replied with the same idea but in completely different words: 'I've a better one, Peig,' she said.

'If so,' says Peig, 'say it.'

Gobnait then began:

> All that will ever come or has come will go away
> But God will never be without mercy.
> You and I will leave this earth
> And leave behind us all we possess.

Having recited the verse she burst out laughing and said: 'I won't leave very much after me because I've very little in this world.' That was the kind of faith which they had. They had it unknown to themselves and the children picked it up with the result that I had little difficulty at all in teaching them either prayers or Catechism.

Another thing about them was that they never forgot the dead. One day a girl brought the following little prayer, if you could call it that, to school from her mother. What a pity the mothers of today who still have these prayers don't do likewise! This is what was written down:

> The law of the graveyard is to allow everyone in.
> The law of the graveyard is to allow no one out.
> Of all who have died no one will ever return.
> Woe is he who doesn't understand his plight
> For no matter how high the tide it recedes again
> And no matter how long the day the night is destined to fall.

It is only now I fully understand it. On looking back over those little poems which I got on the Blasket I notice that in each of them mention is made of the sea or the tide, as in the above verse: 'No matter how high the tide it recedes again.' It was, as you might say, in their blood.

Pádraig Tyers talking to Seán Ó Guithín

T: Seán, what were the reasons for finally making up your minds to abandon the Island completely?

Ó G: Oh well, the main reason, I suppose, was that the people were getting old and no young person growing up except the few who were already there, and it was no place at all for old people. It was like a ship which requires a certain number of crew members. Another reason was that the old people couldn't travel in or out. They were, I suppose, coming to realise that too. They were also tired of the drudgery because they had seen that the old people who went before them had little to show for their efforts most of the time.

Then a young man, Seán Ó Cearnaigh, fell ill. That was just around Christmas-time. He had been in poor health for a while. In any case the weather was bad and he died about twelve o'clock mid-day on the tenth of January 1948 without priest or friar. The day didn't look very good. However four men went out to get all that was required for the wake. Two of them went to Dingle and the other two stayed around Dunquin. They didn't return that night because the coffin wasn't ready and so the two in Dingle had to stay put. When they reached Dunquin the following day no boat could put to sea. The four of them brought everything for the wake down to the pier at the Great Cliff and waited there in the hope that the weather might improve, but it didn't. On the second day it calmed down a little but still it was not calm enough as yet for a nayvogue to come in, so they sent for the lifeboat – we always called it the 'lifeboat' in Irish – to Valentia and asked them to come to remove the corpse.

T: What about the people at home at this time? Did they know what was happening outside?

Ó G: They knew nothing at all about it and were very worried because they were thinking that maybe the nayvogue had tried to make it during the night and that the story was in fact worse, that it was lost at sea. People fear all sorts of things when the weather is bad. However the lifeboat came to Dingle Quay, so the islanders had to carry the coffin and everything else up the Great Cliff again and bring them to Dingle. We were on the

Island and because nobody or no news was coming in and the day was getting mild one man said that if the islanders were short of tobacco they'd go out, it was so nice and mild. They began making a coffin for Seán inside. They had the base laid out on the floor – it was just the right size – when we spotted the boat rounding Slea Head from the east. We had a fairly good idea then that maybe they had got a boat to come from Dingle, and so the work on the coffin ceased. What was it but the lifeboat!

T: Coming from Dingle?

Ó G: Coming from Dingle Quay with the 'wake'. On board were two brothers of the chap who had died, one of whom had travelled out in the nayvogue and the other one who was living in Dublin. However the lifeboat came to the top of the Anvil which is a rock just beside the pier. The coffin was taken off and brought up to the house. It was laid on the floor, the corpse was put into it and it was brought out again to the lifeboat. There wasn't a hope that any nayvogue could put to sea. In fact there was little the islanders could do but bring the coffin out to the top of the Anvil and put it on board the lifeboat. There was a heavy swell inside by the pier. The lifeboat brought the coffin off east to Dingle Quay. The corpse was kept in Dingle that night because an inquest had to be held and on the following day it was brought back again to Dunquin. It was buried there in the old graveyard. From that on the people of the Island were very down and out. Unless you were on the Island that night and the previous day you couldn't realise what a worry it was to have no news from outside, indeed no news in either direction. That really broke the people's heart. They were beginning to see then that they'd be better off clearing out altogether.

T: The fishing, of course, had failed.

Ó G: Oh, the fishing had failed. The mackerel had failed but lobster-fishing was still going on.

T: What about America at that time? Did America have anything to do with the situation?

Ó G: Well, after the war America opened up again and those who had anybody belonging to them over there, a sister or a brother, an uncle or an aunt, were writing to say that they were prepared to go there, and those in America were also writing, I suppose to encourage those at home to leave. Many of them did go over at that time. All that was left then, I imagine, were two nayvogue crews and a handful of old people.

Then De Valera came. I don't know if he was President of Ireland then. After the upset caused by the death of Seán Ó Cearnaigh, the boy who died without priest or friar, Dev visited the Blasket. He was already after visiting all the islands around Ireland. He came to the Blaskets this day, anyhow, and the islanders were down at the pier to meet him. He was talking to them and asking what he could do for them and this old man Maras Ó Catháin – Maras Mhuiris we called him – answered him saying that there was probably nothing to be done for them but take them off the Island, and Dev of course said that there were certain people in Dublin who wouldn't be pleased if that was done. That is what he said.

T: They were people who wished the Island to remain as it was?

Ó G: They were.

T: But they had no connection with the Island?

Ó G: No connection at all.

T: The situation dragged on then from year to year until 1953, didn't it?

Ó G: It did, 1953.

T: I see. And how were things on the Island then? How many people lived there and how many houses were inhabited?

Ó G: When Dev came?

T: No, in 1953.

Ó G: Oh, in 1953 there were only nine houses left, and in three if not four of them there was only one person living alone.

T: And how many people were there all told?

Ó G: About twenty-four or so, I'd say. Yerrah the Island was finished by that time. Going to bed at night you'd know who'd be going to Dunquin next morning, 'going out' as we used to say. Before that there were so many people there that you wouldn't have an idea who was going out next morning. There was always someone who had a reason for going out. As for young people there were really only two nayvogue crews left in 1953.

T: I think that something else then happened on the main-

163

land, the transfer of the Ó Cíomháin family.

Ó G: In 1953 the Ó Cíomháin family was transferred down the country, to Rathcoole in County Kildare.

T: From Ballinaraha?

Ó G: From Ballinaraha in Dunquin. Ulick Moran was transferred too. Their lands were then vacant and two people from the Land Commission came to the Island and told the islanders that if they were prepared to move out they'd get a house and some of the vacant land. The islanders agreed. One of the two was a man named Goulding and the other O'Brien.

T: You yourself were satisfied with the offer?

Ó G: I was, so I was, but I told them that they'd have to give me as much land as would keep a cow, nothing more, nothing less, but they didn't give me as much as would keep her.

T: Were some of the Islanders slow to sign?

Ó G: I wouldn't say so. They could see that they'd soon have to leave of their own accord in any case.

T: There was another reason why one family at any rate wanted to leave. They had a young child.

Ó G: Oh yes. Seán Ó Catháin got married shortly before that and had a son. He'd have to leave the Island to send his son to school. He'd have to go out of his own accord, maybe, but he was happy enough about moving out. Anyway the houses were built outside on the mainland in or around 1952.

T: At the end of the summer, I think.

Ó G: At the end of the summer, I think.

T: How many new houses were built?

Ó G: Four new houses were built, and some of the islanders got the houses of the two who were transferred up country, Ó Cíomháin and Ulick Moran. Seán Ó Catháin got Ulick's house and three islanders were put into Ó Cíomháin's house.

T: Liam Ó Cíomháin's?

Ó G: Liam Ó Cíomháin's house in Ballinaraha. A wall was built to divide it in two and Pádraig Mistéal got one half and Eoghan and Séamas Ó Duinnshléibhe got the other one where the kitchen was. The loft was divided in the same way. A partition was built in the loft so that Eoghan and Séamas got the part over the kitchen and Mistéal got the lower part. A stairs led up to the loft and it was fixed to suit them.

T: Was there much land going with those houses?

Ó G: Four acres of ground we were told but I make out that I haven't any four acres. Then Seán Ó Catháin was put into Ulick Moran's house. Seán left the Island before we did because his son Gearóid had to go to school. We stayed on for a while after.

T: So Seán Cheaist Ó Catháin was the first to move out.

Ó G: He was. When the time came to move Seán was the first to go.

T: That was October 1953, I think.

Ó G: October 1953, indeed it was.

T: Who was the next to leave?

Ó G: The Ó Catháin family, Seán Mharas Mhuiris and one of the Ó Dálaigh men, and my mother too. She came out in the month of November. The houses were built and finished by then, and a ton of coal was delivered to each house beforehand.

T: By the government?

Ó G: By the government. As I said my mother left in the month of November as well as Maras Mhuiris Ó Catháin and his wife and son Seán. They moved into their new house and my mother moved over to my sister in Ballintemple, but my brother Muiris and myself stayed on inside because we had rams on the hill and we wanted to bring them down from the hill and take them out with us. That's how it was. So we stayed on inside and the day we left the Island was the twenty-seventh of December 1953.

T: So ye weren't on the mainland for the Christmas itself?

Ó G: We weren't because it wasn't possible. We thought that we might be out for Christmas Eve but we were inside for the Christmas. We had no oil. We hadn't brought any in because we had intended leaving, so we used whatever drop was there and we hadn't even a candle on Christmas Eve. I'll tell you what we did. You know those slabs of tallow that used to be found on the sea during the war a few years before that? We had one of them in the house so we pared it down with a knife, put it on a saucer and got a cotton wick. We had that too from the time of the war because we used to get bales of cotton on the sea in those days and other bales that were broken maybe in two halves. Anyhow we made a wick from the cotton, melted the tallow on the fire, poured it over the wick and lit it. They were the candles we had on Christmas Eve and Christmas Night. Then we killed a sheep because it was always the custom on the Island to kill a sheep for Christmas. She was one of my own and we had her to eat. We weren't short of food. We had plenty of potatoes and salted fish. We even filled the sheep's puddings because our people before us on the Island always did it.

T: And ye ate them?

Ó G: We did, and what we didn't eat we brought out with us. Upon my soul we ate them. When my mother and Maras Mhuiris and his wife and Seán moved out the only person left in their island home was their son Maras.

T: Maras Mhuiris?

Ó G: Maraisín Mhuiris we used to call him, and my brother Maras and myself told him to move in with us, that the three of us would be company for each other whatever length of time we'd be there.

T: After the others had left?

Ó G: After the others had left, and that's the way it was. He stayed with us there until we moved out after Christmas. Anyhow the weather broke. We thought that we'd be able to come out before Christmas Eve but things don't always turn out as expected, and as I said, the weather broke. Yerrah, the sea-swell was going up on the grass, and there was a gale and showers and then came Christmas Eve. On Christmas Morning we had neither Mass nor service, but we went down to the school where there was a big image or statue of the Virgin Mary. We went and said our Rosary there. From the day the statue came there if ever a Sunday was too wild and the people couldn't go to Mass they'd go down there. The old women never went out to Mass on a Sunday. They'd go down to the statue instead and say the Rosary. That's where we went and said out Rosary, so we did. We had a piece of the sheep, potatoes and so on for the Christmas dinner.

T: I presume that the furniture had been shifted out by this time.

Ó G: The furniture was gone out, all right, although the dresser wasn't. We still had it inside.

T: And how was it brought out?

Ó G: We brought it out in a nayvogue a while later. We had it lying across the nayvogue between the two gunwales.

T: You mean the furniture?

Ó G: The dresser, the dresser.

T: No, I'm talking about the furniture.

Ó G: The furniture was brought out in a nabby from Dingle. Mikie Brosnan from Dingle and his son brought it out and someone else whose name I can't remember. They brought the furniture to Dingle Quay. They intended bringing it to Dunquin and I think they had arranged for a horse in Dunquin to be at the Top of the Cliff to bring it straight to the houses, but the day they had decided on to do so was very bad with a heavy swell going up onto the grass. In any case the nabby arrived. It came to the top of the Anvil the day it was supposed to come. It had no intention of going to Dunquin. Then Peaidí Mhicil and Seán Mharas Mhuiris and myself rowed out to it. It wasn't too pleasant at all inside by the pier. The only good thing about it was that the tide was in because if it was out you couldn't leave the pier at all.

We went out to the nabby anyhow and the two men from the Land Commission came back in with us. We brought them in as far as the island slip. They went up the village and around from house to house and told us that we'd have to go to Dingle to get the keys of the new houses on the mainland. The furniture, beds and other odds and ends were brought out to the top of the Anvil and taken to Dingle.

T: But they needed a nayvogue to do so.

Ó G: Oh a nayvogue was sent out.

T: To the boat?

Ó G: To the nabby, because on account of her size she could not come into the pier at all. We went from there to Dingle Quay where the furniture was unloaded. We stayed in Dingle that night and on the following day it was brought from there to Dunquin on a lorry – a motor-truck as they call it. Each islander removed his own belongings from the lorry into his house.

T: So there was nothing left on the Island only the bare minimum.

Ó G: Nothing at all.

T: When was the furniture brought out, sometime in November?

Ó G: About the end of November, I suppose. That's what I think.

T: You were talking about the dresser a few moments ago.

Ó G: The dresser on which we used to keep the ware was still on the Island and so were the potatoes. Yerrah, I suppose it was into the spring when the days were getting long and the sea was calm by the time we brought the dresser out across the two gunwales of the nayvogue. At the pier at the Great Cliff we laid it down on two nayvogue masts and we tied it to them, and with two of us on either side we brought it up from the pier like you would with a barrow, only that it wouldn't fit on a small barrow. We brought it on a horse and car from the Top of the Cliff to the house and we still have it here.

After my mother, the blessing of God on her soul, and Maras Mhuiris and the two others moved out our only pastime inside was to go west to the Sand-hill. Wild geese were coming in there and that's something they never did while the people were on the Island. Before that they always landed on Beginis and Yellow Island but I suppose they noticed that the people were leaving. Anyhow they started coming to the Sand-hill and we would steal west on them with a gun particularly by moonlight. We killed one of those for Christmas but I didn't find it nice to eat at all. It seemed to me as if the taste of the bog was off it, you understand.

T: Who had the gun?

Ó G: Oh I had.

T: What kind of gun?

Ó G: A single-barrel shot-gun and we made great use of it killing rabbits while I was living on the Island. In summertime we used to go west to the Tearaght killing guillemots with it. We'd shoot them on the sea and it was very handy when we had lobster pots out because if we ran short of bait for the pots and hadn't enough wrasse or other kinds of bait all we had to do was to kill a couple of cormorants, skin them and use them as pot bait. It wasn't of much use as lobster bait but it was great for crabs. Oh it was great crab bait, that is if you wanted to catch a crab. We made great use of the gun on the Island.

T: Well then, the twenty-seventh of December came. Ye got up early that morning, it seems.

Ó G: On Christmas Eve and Christmas Day the weather was miserable and St Stephen's Day wasn't too good either, but on the morning of the twenty-seventh my brother Muiris got up and put his head out the door. He said that the day looked very good and was very calm. Anyhow he started to light the fire. Maraisín Mhuiris was complaining of a bad toothache the previous night because he had the sweat knocked out of him running after sheep on the hill a few days before that. Anyway he had this toothache. Muiris was lighting the fire after getting up. It was pitch dark and he had no proper light only the cresset. I think he had the cresset lighting. I was still in bed myself. The man in the room above was complaining of the toothache, and it wasn't long until I heard my brother Muiris complaining below at the fireplace. 'Begor,' I said, 'there's something wrong with you.' I got out of bed and when I went down what did I see only the hearthstone with a lot of blood on it. What happened was that when he was breaking sticks in the pitch-dark he hit his finger with the hatchet. I'll remember it for a long time. 'Well now,' I said, 'hold on there now together the two of ye.' Myself and Maras Mhuiris got up anyway and Maras tied a piece of cloth around my brother's finger. It was cut fairly badly by the hatchet and when we were up and dressed we went outside the door. It was broad daylight by that time. There was a nayvogue going south past the Cliff Well on its way to Dunquin, the Ó Dálaigh and the Ó Duinnshléibhe men. We went off down to the pier and brought a donkey with us.

T: Ye decided after breakfast that ye would leave?

Ó G: We did, we did after seeing how the morning was.

T: Of course ye had breakfast first.

Ó G: We had. When we got up we said a few prayers and got the breakfast. We made up our minds then to make for Dunquin.

T: Seán, do you remember turning the key in the keyhole?

Ó G: I remember it well, closing the door and saying to myself that many was the fine happy day I went in and out that door, going fishing on bright mornings and coming in good and tired in the evenings, and I said to myself that there was an end to all that now.

T: You were sort of reluctant to leave, were you?

Ó G: I was lonely leaving right enough, but in another way I wasn't because we had a hard life of it there and I knew what was ahead of me, you see. You'd have to be sensible about it. If you stayed on for some years the story would only get worse. We'd be getting older and there would be no place on the mainland for us by then. You'd have to buy a site for a house.

T: In any case ye left the house and the Island behind.

Ó G: We left the house and the Island. There was just one thing, though. I suppose we'd be lonelier after the Island if we were going somewhere out of sight of it, but there isn't a morning in the year when I get up that I don't go back a few steps behind the house and the first place I look at is the Island. I wouldn't even think of looking south towards the Clasach. That meant a lot to us because we had the Island on our doorstep as you might say, just like you'd have a farm on your doorstep and you could go out walking it. We could go in there any time we wanted to and we had our sheep there. We used go shearing them in the beginning of June and spend a fortnight or three weeks there having great fun.

T: What did ye have in the nayvogue coming out that day?

Ó G: We went down then to the slip with a donkey, two rams and, I think, three dogs. We had all those in the nayvogue coming out.

T: And some clothes and things of that sort, I suppose.

Ó G: We had a few clothes. We were after sending out our clothes before that except for a few duds that would do us on the Island. Then we set out on our journey.

T: You said that you saw a nayvogue heading for Dunquin.

Ó G: It was south of the Point's End, in a place called the Cliff Well, which is on this side of the Point, and Muiris saw it that morning when we went outside the house.

T: Those people remained inside longer than yourselves, did they?

Ó G: They were going out for groceries to bring to the Island so that they could stay there another while and not go hungry.

T: They hadn't moved out yet?

Ó G: They hadn't, yet. Tom Daly, that is Tom of the Island, stayed outside on the mainland and his father and Peaidí stayed inside. Anyway on 27 December 1953, as I told you, I left my home there for the last time. The Ó Súilleabháin family and the Ó Duinnshléibhe family stayed for a while after us. The Ó Súilleabháin family didn't move out until the autumn of 1954, I imagine.

T: When ye were coming out ye knew what ye were leaving behind. Did ye know what was ahead of ye?

Ó G: We didn't know what was ahead of us except that we'd be on dry ground and that we could go wherever we wanted of our own accord, that we wouldn't have to call anyone to carry a nayvogue down or up the pier because on the Island you couldn't go for a half-pound of tea, say, without calling on someone to carry the nayvogue down and go out to Dunquin with you. Yerrah, Pádraig, we didn't realise how easy life was on the mainland compared with the Island. There was great hardship on the Island for anyone who had to go through it. No one could understand it only the people of the Island themselves. Suppose now you were setting out to go anywhere tomorrow morning, or suppose you had an animal to bring to the fair you'd have to go up the hill the day before, cut two big bundles of bedding or heather and bring them down to the pier that evening. Then next morning you'd have to put a rope on your cow or your beast and bring her down to the slip. You'd have eight men with you to knock her and put her into the nayvogue. She was knocked on the slip and her four legs were tied. The nayvogue was launched beside the slip and filled with this bedding or heather up above the lower gunwales. Then with everyone giving a hand the cow was put into the nayvogue beside the slip and they'd settle her in as well as they could. Her head was tied to the hole in the row-lock or to the cross-ribs underneath and there was a man in charge of her to watch her head in case she moved. A second nayvogue with four men aboard travelled close to the one carrying the cow which had three men in it. Then they headed for the slip in Dunquin. They had the same commotion there trying to take her out and untie her. If they were bringing her to the bull in Dunquin – it was all bulls in those days – after she was finished with the bull they'd have to drive her down the Great Cliff again and repeat the whole operation below, knocking her and putting her into the nayvogue.

That was what you might call work.

T: Was there any danger that the nayvogue might be damaged or capsized?

Ó G: There was, if the cow was up too high in the nayvogue. I was bringing a cow out one time – she wasn't my own – with two other men. There was another nayvogue travelling with us but it was a good bit away from us. When we were heading for the Great Cliff she started to move. Cattle had the habit of moving when they'd see land. Anyhow this cow started to move. There was too much bedding under her and so she was up too high in the nayvogue. She was slipping to one side but we pulled the bedding away from that side, we settled her down again and reached the quay safe and sound. It could be dangerous if a cow worked herself loose but that never happened because they were tied so securely and as well as that the best of rope was always used. It certainly was dangerous. That was the kind of hardship and trouble that went with life on the Island, but now here in Dunquin I have only to say 'Hoosh out!' to get the cow from the cowhouse out to the field, and say 'Hoosh out!' and bring her out to the bull. I don't have to call anyone. I can do it myself.

T: Seán, even if there was a helicopter or small plane or some such thing servicing the Island when ye were leaving do you think ye would have stayed there?

Ó G: We wouldn't stay at that time, Pádraig. It was twenty years too late by then, or maybe thirty years too late, so it was. For the few people that were left it wasn't worth their while staying on. If they had everything they could ask for it still wouldn't be worth their while staying. I don't think they'd stay.

T: After moving out, Seán, what was the greatest difference ye noticed between life on the Island and life on the mainland?

Ó G: Do you know, we found it strange out here for the first month at any rate. We had nothing in the world to do only walk around the house but if we were on the Island we'd have a hundred things to do. We could go back along the hill. We could go back to Seal Cove. Maybe there might be a few bits of wreckage behind on the Sorrowful Slope and three or four of us would be back there keeping an eye on it and you wouldn't feel the evening passing. I'm talking about wintertime of course. You'd go back the hill, yourself and another lad or two, looking at sheep. A rabbit might jump out and the dog would chase him and if there was anything troubling your mind this would help you to forget it. Then if the day was fine we'd go looking for wreckage in a nayvogue. We used to go setting snares for rabbits, and at night we'd go rambling to some house playing cards and so on. There was always something that would pass the day for us. But when we came out to the mainland we had nothing to do only to be looking at one another.

T: Although ye knew the people of Dunquin well did ye still feel like strangers there?

Ó G: Well, we knew the people of Dunquin because they were our neighbours and they were good to us. When we'd come from Dingle, say, and go down the pier to the nayvogues to row into the Island we might find ourselves held up by bad weather, but they were all very good about giving lodgings to any of us who hadn't any relatives we could stay with. Sometimes we'd go east to Dingle Quay, with a nabby full of sheep and wool and then we'd come by road from Dingle to Dunquin where we'd get a nayvogue and then we'd have to go looking for thole-pins and oars from the locals. They always gave them to us. They were very generous. Still and all when we moved out we felt kind of strange amongst them; but I suppose it was only imagination. Anyway we had nothing to do the first year we came out, that first Christmas and month of January up to the beginning of the spring. By then there was something for us to kill the day. We did a bit of tilling. There was, however, one big difference between Dunquin and the Island. Here in Dunquin you could go off on your own without having to call anyone, but if someone on the Island was sick and needed a priest or a doctor you'd be wondering if tomorrow would be fine, especially if it was the middle of winter. We haven't to put up with that any longer. I can go for a doctor or priest on my own and not bother with anyone else. In the case of people living on the Island the sea was always the master. You could almost say that it was their master even when they were asleep. If you got up in the morning on the Island and the man of the house was still in bed the first word he'd say was what way was the wind blowing. That was the first word, the first salute. If the wind was blowing one way the road would be open and if it was blowing another way there might be a surge or a swell, as they say here, close to land outside at the Great Cliff, so that the sea was always their master. That three miles of sea was like a weight on their hearts. That's all over now.

T: Vanished.

Ó G: Vanished.

T: I suppose ye were very dependent on one another on the Island, Seán.

Ó G: We were. We had to be, and the Islanders were great at helping one another. If you were fighting with me today you'd have to make it up with me tomorrow, whether you liked it or not, and I'd have to make it up with you too because I might need your help the day after that again. They stood by one another in that way. They were great. The time you'd need help most was when cows had to be brought out to the mainland or when a priest or a doctor had to be sent for. There was no question of letting a person down. You went when you got the call.

T: Seán, it is twenty-nine years or more, in fact almost thirty years, since you left the Island. Are there any special thoughts about it that run into your head now?

Ó G: There are, and if there were another twenty years down on top of that the Island will be in my head as long as I live. There was some sort of charm about it that no one could understand except, I suppose, the person who lived there since he was a child. I can't explain what sort of charm it was. Even the coming of each season brought its own charm for us especially when we were young lads. There was the time for making lobster-pots and time for fishing with the pots and then you had the mackerel starting in the autumn. There was always something about it but I can't explain it. We looked forward to it with great delight.

T: Are you sorry that you didn't emigrate to America?

Ó G: No, not now, although there was a time when I wanted to go, but what I wanted most was to join the guards, so it was. I applied to join along with two others from the Island. We got a form and we went north to the Garda Barracks in Ballyferriter. We filled it up and did all that we had to do. The form was sent to Dublin, I suppose. We were to do an examination after filling the form. It was a year after that, I imagine, before we were called, and myself and one of the two others with me were over-age by then.

T: Because the year had passed?

Ó G: Yes. I suppose we were within a year of the age limit.

T: When ye applied?

Ó G: Yes.

T: I suppose, Seán, that the people of the Island are often in your mind and you often think of them.

Ó G: They are, often. Sometimes I'm in the house at night-time and if I shut my eyes they are as fresh as could be in my head. I see them working. I hear Maras Mhuiris saying 'Hie out!' to the donkey, and I see them lobster-fishing and making pots and so on. I feel that they aren't dead at all. The Island will always be in my mind. I'll always be thinking of it. Still I prefer to be out here now.

T: Do you think the day will come when people will again settle down permanently on the Island?

Ó G: That will depend on how the world goes. You can't tell how the world might change. People were there before and you never know, they might go there again. But no matter who goes there they'll never be as good as the islanders at handling the problems that go with life there. I wouldn't think so, especially as regards nayvogues. The islanders were such experts at handling nayvogues. They were like cats in them. They were experts at handling them at sea as well as carrying them down and up the slip. And as for coming ashore in the various inlets and taking sheep off Beginis and things like that I don't think that anyone who might come to live there could do it, although the gear nowadays is much better. They have motor-boats to work the Island, still I don't think they could work the Island like the islanders did.

T: Seán, after all the years you spent on the Island do you regard the sea as an enemy?

Ó G: I'd say it is. I suppose it is the enemy of every boatman especially on a bad day, but yet when we were living there no matter what hardship you went through, as we often did coming out to Dunquin or going lobster-fishing and so on, when you put the nayvogue up on its stand and secured it you left all your troubles beneath it. You'd think no more of it then, you'd leave the day's worries and all the hardship you suffered inside there under the nayvogue.

T: Cáit, where are you from originally?

M: Well, the townland they call Derryartha is where I was born.

T: Near Carraroe, is it?

M: In Carraroe. When I was young my father kept me at home from school one time to give him a couple of days' help working in the field. Begor on the third day didn't the guard come and ask me why I wasn't at school. I quickly told him that my father kept me at home to help him pulling seaweed.

'Well,' he said in English, 'you'll be at school tomorrow?'

I didn't understand a word he said.

'I have no English,' I said to him.

'Oh, my!' he said in Irish, 'I hope you'll be in school tomorrow.'

'I will,' I said, and the next thing was that I took to my heels and went ahide.

T: Who was the guard?

M: Muiris Ó Súilleabháin. Anyhow life went on as usual. A couple of years later I gave up school. This particular winter a cookery class started in Carraroe. I went there and the teacher we had was Mrs Hipwell-Joyce. I think she was English and the classes were given in English. I don't know from God down how she happened to come to the area but our parish priest made it known that he would like the young girls to have something to keep them off the roads and away from the kitchen rackets, as they were called.

T: What were the kitchen rackets?

M: A sort of céilí or dance in the houses.

T: Ball nights as they call them in the West Kerry Gaeltacht?

M: Ball nights, but kitchen rackets was what they were called in Connemara. In those days the local boys had nowhere to go except to Carraroe Crossroad, and when we used to come out from the cookery classes no matter what we had made, a rhubarb pie or a blackberry pie or something else, the lads would ask us for a bit of it and if they didn't get it they'd take it off us. Anyhow the teacher complained to the guards. One night I was going home after the class. I had a rhubarb pie and this lad – I don't know who he was because it was dark, about ten o'clock at night – made a drive at me to snatch a piece of the pie from me. Didn't the guard walk over, he caught him by the shoulder and said to him: 'Go home, boy!'

Then he said to me: 'I'll go with you to the top of the road.'

We stood there talking for a while. 'I'd go another bit of the road now with you,' said he, 'but I must go home.'

That's all right, boy,' I said.

'But,' he said, 'I'll see you some night during the week.' So I continued on with the cookery and Ó Súilleabháin used to meet me and walk me home.

T: Was Carraroe the first place Muiris was stationed after he joined the guards?

M: It wasn't. Inverin was the first place he was sent. I don't know if he was a full year there when he was transferred to Carraroe in 1927 or 1928.

T: You knew nothing about the Blasket at that stage?

M: Oh I knew nothing from God down about it, my dear.

T: What did the local people think of you going out with a guard?

M: I was trying to do it on the quiet because I was afraid, you understand. For example there was a speak-easy less than three-quarters of a mile from our house. If they saw me talking to Ó Súilleabháin or to any other one of the guards and then if the guards raided that house at night and found anything I was surely the one who told them and I was in trouble. I'd get my reckoning if that happened.

T: Do you remember finding out that Muiris was from the Blasket?

M: I do, but I thought, God save us, that the Blasket was so far away and so far out to sea that he might as well have been from that place where the Mau Maus live. Anyhow time was passing like that until 1934 and then he asked me would I marry him. Of course I said I would because to give him his due he was a fine block of a man, over six feet high and fifteen stone in weight.

T: Of course he had resigned from the guards before ye got married?

M: He had. He resigned from the guards on 5 July 1934 just five days before we got married.

T: Why did he resign?

M: He never liked the guards. He really hated them, not the men themselves but the work. The Connemara people, you understand, were very like the Blasket people, and there was nothing he hated more than getting up at night or at the dawn of day and going out to some far-away townland, out to Lettermore, say, or out to Muckinagh or some place like that, breaking into a house and starting to ransack it, tearing beds apart and throwing people out of their beds. He hated that work like hell.

Anyhow we married on 10 July 1934 in Killeen Church in Carraroe and off we went as far as Galway. God be merciful to Seán Ó Catháin, it was he who took us there in his car because he was a member of the County Council and had to attend the meetings every Saturday. We had our breakfast in McMahon's Hotel and from there we went to the Royal Hotel where Muiris had arranged to meet friends of his. People were coming and going and my brother and my aunt's family were with us.

We had decided to come to Carrig west of Dingle on our honeymoon. It was getting late and the train would soon be leaving. A doctor from Carraroe – his name was Tubridy – came to the hotel and took us down to the train. We got on the train. It was then the loneliness hit me and I thought that I'd never again see Carraroe or Galway. Of course I knew as little as the thrush that soars up into the sky about honeymoons or marriage or anything else. All I knew was that I was married.

Anyhow we got into Limerick. It was about seven o'clock in the evening by then and the weather was the finest that ever came since, I suppose, but about ten o'clock it started to rain. After breakfast next morning we went by train to Tralee. We had a meal there and then got the train to Dingle. We'd have walked it while the train was coming from Tralee to Dingle. I think the journey took four hours.

T: By the way what put it into your head to come to Carrig?

M: Muiris' sister was married to Pádraig Ó Cíomháin in Carrig. He was known as Peaidí Tom from Clogher. They married in America in 1930, I think, and I don't know how long they were married before they came home.

Well when I got into Dingle I thought that there was no poor woman amongst my relatives. Muiris' sister Máire and her husband were waiting for us – God be good to them, they have all gone the way of truth – with a big red cart and a big bay horse. We settled ourselves into the cart but Muiris was very stout and wouldn't get into it. He said that he'd walk a part of the way. It was only when we were coming up the Long Road that he sat in, and from that on we didn't stop until we came to Carrig.

T: That was your first time in this side of the country?

M: That was my first time ever seeing Kerry and when I saw that we were going west, west, west: 'Oh, God and Mary be with us,' I said, 'this place is as far back as the food in the periwinkle. I thought,' I said to myself, 'that I was far enough west when I was in Carraroe but the devil and all is on this place.' Of course when I got to Carrig I couldn't understand a word of what the people were saying. I felt a right fool. I had some English but what good was that? There wasn't a word of English to be heard in that house, nothing at all only Irish. In the end I understood the words 'May your marriage succeed!' but it took me a long time because that is not what Connemara people say but 'May you enjoy your new life'.

T: Cáit, do you remember your first visit to the Blasket while you and Muiris were in Carrig?

M: I do. It was a Sunday morning. A boat from Dingle was leaving Ballincolla for the Island. Three of us, myself and Muiris and Seán Ó Dubhda, may the Lord have mercy on them, left Carrig. We went down to the shore, down through the mud and seaweed, and got into the boat. Muiris had a bottle of whiskey that he had bought in Ballyferriter on his way west, and Master Ó Dubhda had another bottle for the journey. I suppose we were half-way to the Island when everyone began to get sick and Muiris was handing the bottle around from one person to another, and so was Master Ó Dubhda. It wasn't long until Ó Dubhda's bottle was empty and he stuck the cork into it. 'Oh, my, Muiris,' he said, 'I think the whole lot of them are getting sick.'

The next thing was we were near the Island and the boat veered south. A nayvogue came out and we had to get into it. That's when the chattering started. You'd think they were wild geese with everyone talking. In we went. 'May your marriage succeed!' 'Oh my! Isn't she a peach!' 'How are you, Méin?' and 'How are you, Máire?' and so on.

They took Muiris away with them and drowned him with tears and dried him with kisses. I didn't know where he was in the end. After a while we walked up to the village. Muiris' brother, known as the Tailor, was there to meet us in Seán Eoghain's house where he was living since Muiris' people left their own home known as the House on the Slope. A drop of tea was made and there were women coming to talk to Muiris and I didn't know from God down who they were. Then the two of us went up to the House on the Slope. There was a little low fence outside it. I sat down on the fence. Muiris stayed for a while looking up at the house and then he crossed over the fence. There was a great big lock on the door. He looked in through the window. He walked back out again and sat on the fence. The next thing was he put his head under him and started crying. I was looking at him, 'Well, Muiris,' I said, 'there's no good in this. You know what happened.'

The house was empty and, God help us, I suppose many thoughts ran into his head.

'Come on,' I said, 'we'll go back the hill or somewhere.'

'We'll go up to Seán Mhicil,' he said.

Sure enough Seán and his wife were at home, and Mary and Lís and Seáinín. Seáinín took down the fiddle, Muiris got another one and we had some music. We were chatting for a while and we took some photographs. It was only a day's visit. We came out again that evening.

T: Did you get the impression that Muiris was lonely leaving?

M: Oh, indeed he was lonely in there.

T: Ye paid other visits to the Island again afterwards, I suppose.

M: We went in one more time after that, after Christmas I think, in the year 1935. We met Tom Daly and Peaidí on the slip. They were after coming in from the mainland and they had flour and bran and yellow meal and tea and sugar and a lot of other things in the nayvogue.

'Will you let her land?' they asked Muiris.

'I will, of course,' said Muiris.

'Will you come in yourself?'

'I won't,' he said. 'I suppose I'll never again set the soles of my feet on the place.'

T: And did he?

M: He didn't.

T: Cáit, do you think that that was his last visit?

M: It was.

T: Do you think he had any notion of returning to the Island if he lived?

M: I don't think so, but he spent his life writing, Pádraig. Do you know what he had in mind? He wanted a bridge to be built from the mainland into the Island and he wrote to every public representative and to everyone else who he thought had influence. If a bridge was built he wouldn't even wait for the sound of his feet to go back there again. I often told him that he was only wasting postage stamps, that all the money in America wouldn't build a bridge there.

T: Talking about the last time both of you went to the Island and he wouldn't set foot on it, do you think he felt that life on the Island was finished or would soon be finished?

M: He knew well that it was.

T: That saddened him, I presume.

M: It did. It made him depressed and the day we went there it really depressed him. He felt, you understand, that there was nobody belonging to himself there.

T: The link was broken?

M: The link was broken. That's the way to say it, Pádraig.

T: How long did ye stay in Carrig?

M: We stayed about eight months.

T: What kind of livelihood did Muiris take up after he resigned from the guards?

M: Writing. While we were in Carrig he decided to write the life of Dónall Cháit Bhillí. Dónall lived back in the Mill in Dunquin, and Muiris spent, I think, six or seven weeks going back and forth to Dónall. I went with him sometimes. He finished the manuscript in Carrig. Of course Muiris' intention was to stay in Kerry and it is a great pity that he didn't, but I suppose what's to be will be.

We were living away in Carrig but I wasn't too happy, you understand. I felt I was in a strange place far away from home and I still wasn't getting used to the dialect. Life wasn't the same in Galway as in this side of the country. People got up early here and you had cows to milk and butter was being made too. Of course I had nothing to do with that. I felt I was fenced in. We had no place of our own and I was in other people's way. I was still worrying about my home place and my people. Muiris intended buying a piece of land, but I felt that no islander, no man of the sea, had much business of land, and anyway Muiris didn't belong to this world. 'What business has an islander of land?' I said to him. 'All he has in his head is fishing and a nayvogue. You don't know your left hand from your right.'

So we made up our minds to move and we left Carrig on 14 March 1935. I was pregnant at the time. We went to Galway and I stayed with my aunt. After a while we built a house in Cullane, a townland within ten minutes' walk of Carraroe. Seán Ó Catháin built it for us and indeed he wasn't long building it. On the third day of the first month of winter a son was born to us in a private hospital in Galway known as Seamount. Muiris never asked me what name we'd give the child. He just said that he'd give him his grandfather's name, Eoghan Ó Súilleabháin.

We came home, Eoghan and myself, and life was treating us all right but I don't think that Muiris was too happy with himself. He was after polishing up the life of Dónall Cháit Bhillí and sending it to a printer but it was all in vain. He then turned around and prepared it in the form of a short story. Still it was all in vain. The manuscript was coming and going to different people and in the end he got sick of it and threw it aside.

T: Of course, he had written *Twenty Years A-Growing* and it had been published before ever ye got married.

M: That's true. He brought *Twenty Years A-Growing* out in 1933.

T: Seoirse Mac Tomáis, otherwise known as George Thomson, was closely connected with that book.

M: He was.

T: When or how did Muiris and Seoirse meet for the first time?

M: Muiris told me that they met inside on the Island. He

183

said that Seoirse was going to school in London and came over to Cork. I don't think he was any more than fourteen or fifteen years of age at the time. He got a lift from Cork to Dingle. The day was pelting rain and there was a gale and a storm blowing. He was going down the street when a man called him. I can't say who that man was but Seoirse himself knows who he was. Seoirse was drenched wet and this man told him to come in. When the rain eased off a bit Seoirse went out again. He met someone or other and enquired how he could get to the Island. He was told that there were people from the Island in Dingle to buy supplies for Hallowe'en. It seems that he found out where Muiris' father was and decided to go with him back to the Island.

T: Seoirse had Irish at that stage?

M: He had only very little. Muiris told me that he met him on the hill the following day. When he was going for a load of turf there was this young man looking across at South Kerry. The first question he asked Muiris, in English, was: 'What's the name of that place to the south?' Muiris told him. Then Seoirse came over and the two of them sat down, pulled out a cigarette and had a smoke. Seoirse came back down home with Muiris. That was in 1916 or 1917 and from then on I may as well say that Seoirse was a genuine friend right down to this very day.

T: He is still alive, isn't he?.

M: He is. He's living in a place called Moseley, Birmingham, with his wife and their eldest daughter.*

T: While Muiris was writing *Twenty Years A-Growing* I think that Seoirse was working in University College Galway.

M: He was, and he was staying in Corrib Lodge, a nice place. Muiris would often call to see him, maybe once a fortnight, but after a while Seoirse got a job in Birmingham University and he remained there until he retired on pension.

T: It was he who translated Muiris' book into English.

M: It was, himself and Moya Llewellyn Davies.

T: Who was Moya Llewellyn Davies?

M: I think she was one of the O'Connors from Newtownmountkennedy. She was married to Crompton Davies. He had a job in England. I'm not sure now if he was a lawyer. I think he was. They had two children, Richard and Kathleen, and they are in England now. I think Richard's wife's name is Lady Llewellyn Davies, and she is involved in politics.

T: But Moya herself is dead, isn't she?

M: She is. She was only fifty, I imagine, when she died.

T: Incidentally did you know when you were courting Muiris that he had already written *Twenty Years A-Growing?*

M: I didn't. Muiris was a very secretive man and he didn't like anyone to know what he was doing until he had done it. Of course the poor man was unlucky because after the book was translated into German the war broke out and the book was burned in Hanover. It came out afterwards, though, in German.

T: Has the book been translated into many other languages since?

M: It was translated into French and into Hindu, and I can't say how many other translations were made of it.

T: After Muiris, as you've said, threw the life of Dónall Cháit Bhillí aside, what did he do?

M: He said it was time to write *Twenty Years in Bloom*. He started where he finished *Twenty Years A-Growing*. He described how he met me and he described the Connemara people, especially the people of Carraroe, and of course the people he loved to spend a day with, those living in Muckinagh. He spent a very long time working on the book and when it was finished he sent it to the printers, but where was the point? The report he got back was that it was too like *Twenty Years A-Growing*. He made some changes in it but even that wasn't enough. Then he sent it to Seoirse and I think Seoirse expressed the same opinion. The war was on at the time. Seoirse left Birmingham and moved the children down to Wales, I think, and a part of the manuscript was either lost or went astray so that was that. Some time afterwards Muiris got a very old book, *The Life of St Elizabeth of Hungary*, from some friend of his in Lettermuckoo. He translated it into Irish and I know where the manuscript is.

T: It was never published?

M: It was never published.

T: Muiris also wrote many articles, I think.

M: Oh, he did. He wrote a lot of articles for the *Irish Press* and he wrote for *Ar Aghaidh* and the *Messenger of the Sacred Heart*.

T: Can you tell me what year he joined the guards for the

second time?

M: He left home to join the guards the second time about 11 March 1950 and he was in the force from then until only 25 July that same year.

T: Why do you think he decided to rejoin after fifteen years or so? Was it that he was fed up of writing by then?

M: Well, I suppose he was thinking of himself, that he was not as lucky then with his writing as he was with the first book, and of course when he wrote the first book he hadn't a care or a worry in the world. The cradle was far from the fire then. Now he was married with two children and a house and no job, and maybe a lot of what he had earned was being spent with nothing coming in to replace it. When Máirín was born he asked me what name we would give her. Said I to him: 'I'm leaving that to yourself.'

'Do you mind, Cáit,' said he, 'if I give her Moya Llewellyn's name?'

'I don't,' I said. So she was called Máire Llewellyn Ní Shúilleabháin. That settled that and I didn't object.

Of course I was keeping visitors in Carraroe and it was very very hard, Pádraig. The house itself was too small. It had only four bedrooms. There was no electric light then and no running water. We had to cut turf and save it, and, you know yourself, it was hard enough on Muiris who never took a turf-spade in his hand. Still and all he managed. There was only a small income from *Twenty Years A-Growing* because the war was on, and in the end Muiris said that there was nothing for him to do but join the guards again. He hoped that he'd be sent to the Aran Islands and that he wouldn't have long to go until he retired on pension. If he went to Aran, of course, everything would be fine, but it wasn't to be. He was sent to Oughterard. Máirín and myself stayed on in Carraroe. Eoghan got a scholarship to the Vocational School in Rosmuck and was staying in Kylesalia.

We had decided to leave Carraroe and go to Oughterard and get someone to rent our own house, but before that happened Muiris came home one day and when he walked into the kitchen: 'Indeed Cáit,' he said to me, 'I never knew that we had such a nice clean house. I never noticed it.' He stayed at home that night and went off again next day. That was his last night at home. On the following Saturday night I woke up out of my sleep. Our young daughter Máirín was sleeping with me. Whatever happened I became really frightened and I was so bad that I had to get up and go downstairs. I wasn't getting any better. I felt as if I was losing consciousness. I went upstairs again and got into bed with Máirín. She was about six years at the time and was due to make her First Communion any day. Of course her father was delighted. He was so fond of the child that I never had to do much for her because as soon as night fell he'd take her upstairs. He'd give her a board and paper and pen and get her to write. Since she was a year old she used to write all the time until she fell asleep.

The day she was due to make her First Communion Muiris intended coming home to see her but something happened in Oughterard and he couldn't make it. After Mass was over and Máirín had made her Communion I hired a car and the two of us went to Oughterard. I brought Máirín in to where Muiris was staying. After a while we went back to Galway again to the pictures in the Savoy, and I'll always remember the picture that was being shown, *They Died with their Boots On.* We brought Muiris back to Oughterard and Máirín and myself came home.

I don't know now if it was the following Saturday that there was a strike on in Galway and Muiris was transferred there. That was 24 July, and the poor fellow went to confession that evening. He received Holy Communion on Sunday morning and had his breakfast in the barracks in Salthill. He was mad for swimming and took his togs with him. He never stopped until he got to the strand known as Lovers' Strand. He went swimming though he had little idea as to what way the current was flowing there. It seems that there was an undercurrent and he was being pulled out to sea all the time. He managed to swim back in but when the poor man stood up he got a weakness, he fell and he was suffocated in three inches of water.

It was a warm day. I sensed that something was going to happen because I had this dream on the Saturday night. Whatever came over me I couldn't get rid of it and Máirín and myself went for a walk. We weren't long back home after the walk, about three o'clock in the afternoon, when a guard came to the house. I noticed clearly the colour of him coming in the gate. He was a friend of mine. I have an idea he was a Corkman, Guard Ó Céilleachair. He walked in, the poor man.

'Well, Mrs Ó Súilleabháin,' he said, 'I'm afraid I have bad news for you.'

I looked at him, and the next thing he said was: 'Muiris is drowned'.

I went numb. The child began to cry and I didn't know where I was. I know that my aunt, the Lord have mercy on her, had to come along with her sisters Máire and Sorcha, and they calmed me down somehow or other. 'There's no doubt,' I said, 'life is very hard on me.'

My mother died when I was, I think, seven years of age. That was hard enough but this was a much bigger blow. Muiris and I were very loving towards one another, we were fond of one another and any disagreement we ever had we got over it and there wasn't another word about it. So Muiris was buried on 27 July 1950.

T: Cáit, where is he buried, the blessing of God on him?

M: He's buried in Killeen graveyard in a place they call Barraderry, nearly three miles from Carraroe, down beside the sea where there's nothing from God down to disturb him but the birds of the strand and the sound of the waves. When he was alive he'd often go there on a Sunday and he'd often go there too on a moonlit night and sit down listening to the sound of the sea. I think he used to feel that he was back again on the Island.

So the funeral was over and everyone went his own way. Eoghan, the poor fellow, returned to Rosmuck. Máirín and myself were on our own. My friend Seoirse Mac Tomáis came over from England and spent a week with me. Then he left. Everyone had to go his own way and I had to plough or drive. I was still a young woman and Muiris was only forty-seven at the time, and the way it is with a person like me or like any other woman whose husband dies young, if you put your head under you and die you're a great woman. If you hold your head high they'll say something else.

I stayed four years in Carraroe. I am not a bit slow or ashamed to say that I got a pension of nine pounds a month from the Minister for Justice. Any person would find it hard to live on that much. I went to work to make extra money. Life was getting harder. 'Well,' I said in my own mind, 'there's no use trying to plough or drive in this place.' There was no opportunity there. Eoghan passed the examination for the Preparatory Colleges and went to school in Coláiste Éanna in Galway. I brought Máirín here to Carrig and from there she attended the Presentation Convent School in Dingle.

I went to England myself and got work there, but if I did it was hard going. It is all right to go there when you're young but when you're a bit old it is hard to get used to it. It was lonely enough too.

T: Is that where you met Pádraig Ó Maoilchiaráin?

M: It is. Pádraig, a native of Inishbarra, was living in England. We met and got married. He's a good man who never left me hungry or thirsty from the day I met him until the present day. He was polite and gentle and quiet. A good man in a boat, on a strand or on a lorry or anything else he sets out to do. He took care of myself and Máirín and our second daughter whose name is Kathie. She was born in England.

T: Did you yourself pay any visit to the Island since Muiris died?

M: I did, five or six years ago, and I suppose it was my last ever visit. I thought the place looked terrible, all the houses fallen down except a few at the top of the village, nothing to be seen, no welcome for anyone at a door or on a hill or on a cliff, nothing but the seagulls. There's no doubt the seagulls have it to themselves at last. And I wonder why it's gone to rack and ruin. Three people came from the Island who brought it fame and renown and it is a great pity that it has been abandoned like that.

I went back along the White Strand but if I did I didn't notice the slip that had been built there. Muiris often spoke of Pádraig Ó Dálaigh and Ceaist and the rest of them, God be merciful to them, and how they used to go down to the slip at night where the dances were held. But that was all over now. There was nothing to be seen in the fields but rabbit burrows and mushrooms.

I sat down on the White Strand and cried my fill. I could see the House on the Slope to the south of me with nothing left of it but the four walls. I'm sad that it's gone and it's a great pity, but that's life.

FOOTNOTES

p. 34 In 1975 two men from the parish of Ballyferriter, Ger Ó Cíobháin and Dónall Mac Síthigh, travelled around the coast of Ireland in a nayvogue. Ger himself gives a detailed account of that voyage in his book *Cogarnach ár gCósta*.

p. 43 Of the two schools one was Catholic and the other Protestant. Irish was taught in the Protestant school and the reading book used began with the sentence: 'Tá an cat breac', i.e. The cat is speckled.

p. 92 Séamus Ó Duilearga was editor of *Béaloideas (The Journal of the Folklore of Ireland Society)* and Professor of Folklore at University College Dublin.

p. 112 Fionán Mac Coluim (1875-1966), a native of Co. Antrim, spent a long period as Irish Language organiser for the Gaelic League in Munster. In later years he was an inspector of Irish.

p. 116 *An Seabhac* whose real name was Pádraig Ó Siochfhradha was born near Dingle. He was a very famous Irish scholar and editor of *An tOileánach*.

p. 153 *Thar Bealach Isteach* and *Peats na Baintreabhaighe*.

p. 154 Piaras was hanged in Killarney in 1653.

p. 184 Seoirse who was Professor of Classics in Birmingham University died on the third of February 1987.

More Interesting Books

THE WILD ROVER
THE AUTOBIOGRAPHY OF
TOMÁS Ó CINNÉIDE
Translated into English by
PÁDRAIG TYERS

Tomás Ó Cinnéide was one of the West Kerry Gaeltacht's best known and most widely travelled sons. He was in his time clerical student, army officer, teacher, postman, American emigrant, factory worker, library sweeper, down-and-out in Skid Row and seanchaí. His story is told with refreshing honesty and humour. The flavour and eloquence of the original Irish have been magically preserved in a fitting translation by Pádraig Tyers.

MÉINÍ
THE BLASKET NURSE
LESLIE MATSON

This is the life story of a remarkable woman, Méiní Dunlevy. Born in Massachusetts of Kerry parents, Méiní was reared in her grandparents' house in Dunquin. When she was nineteen, she eloped with an island widower to the Great Blasket, where she worked as a nurse and midwife for thirty-six years. Returning widowed to Dunquin, she died in 1967, aged 91.

Méiní's story, recorded by the author from her own accounts and those of her friends and relatives in Dunquin, is an evocation of a forceful, spicy personality and a compelling reconstruction of a way of life that has exercised an enduring fascination for readers. *Méiní, the Blasket Nurse* is a worthy successor to *An t-Oileánach* and *Twenty Years a-Growing*.

LETTERS FROM THE GREAT BLASKET
EIBHLÍS NÍ SHÚILLEABHÁIN

This selection of *Letters from the Great Blasket*, for the most part written by Eibhlís Ní Shúilleabháin of the island to George Chambers in London, covers a period of over twenty years. Eibhlís married Seán Ó Criomhthain – a son of Tomás Ó Criomhthain, An tOileánach (The Islandman). On her marriage she lived in the same house as the Islandman and nursed him during the last years of his life which are described in the letters. Incidentally, the collection includes what must be an unique specimen of the Islandman's writing in English in the form of a letter expressing his goodwill towards Chambers.

Beginning in 1931 when the island was still a place where one might marry and raise a family (if only for certain exile in America) the letters end in 1951 with the author herself in exile on the mainland and 'the old folk of the island scattering to their graves'. By the time Eibhlís left the Blasket in July 1942 the island school had already closed and the three remaining pupils 'left to run wild with the rabbits'.

IN MY FATHER'S TIME
EAMON KELLY

In My Father's Time invites us to a night of storytelling by Ireland's greatest and best loved seanchaí, Eamon Kelly. The fascinating stories reveal many aspects of Irish life and character. There are tales of country customs, matchmaking, courting, love, marriage and the dowry system, emigration, American wakes and returned emigrants. The stream of anecdotes never runs dry and the humour sparkles and illuminates the stories.